# GIOVANNI GENTILE ON THE EXISTENCE OF GOD

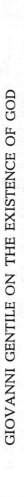

PHILOSOPHICAL QUESTIONS SERIES



No. 1. S.A. Matczak, Ph. D., *Le Problème de Dieu dans la pensée de Karl Barth*. Louvain: Editions Nauwelaerts, 1968.

No. 2. —, *Research and Composition in Philosophy*. Louvain: Editions Nauwelaerts, 1968.

No. 3. —, *Philosophy: A Select, Classified Bibliography of Ethics, Economics, Law, Politics, Sociology*. Louvain: Editions Nauwelaerts, 1970.

No. 4. —, *Philosophy: Its Nature, Methods, and Basic Sources*. In press.

No. 5. —, *Philosophy: Its Histories, Systems and Specific Settings*. To be published.

No. 6. M.R. Barral, Ph. D., *Progressive Neutralism: A Philosophical Aspect of American Education*. Louvain: Editions Nauwelaerts, 1970.

No. 7. W. Smith, Ph. D., *Giovanni Gentile on the Existence of God*. Louvain: Editions Nauwelaerts, 1970.

Others will follow

Library of Congress Catalog No. 70 - 111087
LEARNED PUBLICATIONS, INC.
New York

PHILOSOPHICAL QUESTIONS SERIES

7

WILLIAM A. SMITH

DOCTOR OF PHILOSOPHY

ASSOCIATE PROFESSOR OF PHILOSOPHY

SETON HALL UNIVERSITY

NEW JERSEY, U.S.A.

# GIOVANNI GENTILE ON THE EXISTENCE OF GOD

ÉDITIONS NAUWELAERTS
2, Place Mgr Ladeuze
LOUVAIN

BÉATRICE-NAUWELAERTS
4, rue de Fleurus
PARIS (VIe)

1970

# PREFACE

With great satisfaction our Editing Board presents the study by Professor William Smith on Giovanni Gentile's concept of our knowledge of God's existence. The question of God, paramount in philosophy as well as in every man's social and private conduct, is explored by Gentile in a specific way and with profound insight. His work merits close scrutiny; this Dr. Smith has done, yet leaving room for further examination. Thus both studies, Gentile's and Smith's, are timelessly stimulating and valuable.

Moreover, in the ecumenical age, the investigations of God's existence and our concept of Him present a specific momentum. Inquiry about all man's concepts, even those of the pagan world, needs to be considered from new and revised perspectives. Gentile and Smith serve this need by putting into evidence both various ways whereby God is attainable, and various concepts of Him, deriving from His infinite reality on the one hand and our finitude on the other.

Our *Philosophical Series* has as one of its purposes to assess the answers which powerful minds have found for universal questions and Dr. Smith's study of Gentile's position laudably penetrates that path.

Sebastian A. Matczak
Editor

New York

# TABLE OF CONTENTS

# INTRODUCTION

Giovanni Gentile was one of the most original thinkers that Italy produced in the twentieth century. Gentile was born May 29, 1875[1], in Castelvetrando (Trapani) on the island of Sicily. He studied philosophy at the Regia Scuola Normale Superiore at Pisa and received his doctoral degree in 1897 with a dissertation on Rosmini and Gioberti. In 1898 he became a professor of philosophy at the liceo of Campobasso and Naples and remained there until 1906. He held the chair of history of philosophy at the University of Palermo from 1907 to 1914, when he replaced one of his intellectual mentors at the University of Pisa, Donato Jaja. Jaja died in 1914. He had been a follower and communicator of the thought of the Italian neo-Hegelian idealist, Bertrando Spaventa (1817-1883), who, as we shall see in Chapter Five, had a great influence on Gentile's thought. In 1918 Gentile became professor of philosophy at the University of Rome and held this post until shortly before his death.

Gentile's life, however, was not uniquely devoted to the classroom. During his years of teaching he also carried on extensive lecturing and writing on his new philosophical system. For years he carried on a running dialogue with Benedetto Croce. Besides the discussion of philosophical problems, it was their intention to renew an interest in Italian culture. Much of this writing was done in the journal *La critica,* founded in 1903. Gentile founded his own review, *Giornale critico della filosofia italiana* in 1920.

[1] This is the date given in the *Enciclopedia Italiana,* but another source, *Collier's Encyclopedia,* gives it as May 30.

When Mussolini came to power in 1922, Gentile agreed to write a philosophical doctrine for him; Croce refused. Their friendship never regained its original vigor after this break. During the formation of the Grand Fascist Council, Gentile was asked to become the Minister of Education. Gentile accepted and retained this position from 1922 through 1924 and from 1925 through 1929. During these years he wrote on educational philosophy and fascism. He also brought about a reform in the educational system in Italy, the first since the Casati laws in 1859. Gentile was a senator of the King and a member of the committee on the reform of the constitution of the state. He also edited the Italian Encycopedia. He was founder of the *Instituto nazionale fascista di cultura* and edited its journal *Educazione fascista.*

At least three events greatly saddened Gentile's life. Gentile did not favor the concordat between Italy and the Vatican, since he did not feel that a religious organization should be able to make demands upon the State. Mussolini, however, could only see the practical benefits. Gentile also objected to Mussolini's link with Hitler in the late thirties, but again Mussolini was led on by the practical advantages. Toward the end of his life Gentile lost his son Giovanni, and this led him to insert his thoughts on death and immortality at the end of his last book, *Genesi e struttura della società,* published in 1943.

On april 19, 1944, Gentile was returning from interceding with the police for some students when he was killed on the streets of Florence. Communist partisans have been blamed for the murder. At the time of his death he was still working for the advancement of Fascist culture.

Gentile now seems to have overcome the ill repute which attended his aid to the fascist cause. His philosophy is now the object of intensive study in Italy. A large group of philosophers have contributed to the literature on Gentile. A Foundation of Gentilian Studies (Fondazione Giovanni Gentile per gli studi filosofici) has been established. Professor Ugo Spirito is the present President of the Foundation. This Foundation has established a collection of works on Gentile entitled:

*Giovanni Gentile: La vita e il pensiero.* Ten volumes have been published thus far.[2]

This study will consider the problem of the existence of God in Gentile's thought. It is a major, perennial philosophical problem, one which is pragmatically meaningful and holds a personal fascination. It would be wrong to assert that this problem was the primary one which occupied Gentile's endeavours. Although not primary, the problem of God is a central problem in Gentile's thought. Gentile was mainly concerned with an overall reform of logic and metaphysics as it had come down to us from Greek philosophy. He wanted men to recognize the act of thinking as a pure act within which all being is resolved or synthesized. Reality must be viewed as logocentric-even the unique religious reality, God. As Gentile proceeds, the role of human thinking takes on major importance. Each man comes to be authentically viewed as a spiritual reality, and all objects are viewed as objective moments of his spiritual act, which is thinking. It is evident, therefore, that Gentile's view of reality gives great value to man.

It is a matter of historical record that Gentile's exposition of what he called «actualism» led many to conclude that he had denied the existence of God because he made God to be real only when thought of by man. These critics pointed out that he referred to man's thinking as «pure act,» thereby identifying man with God or making God immanent to human thought. Gentile did not want himself thought of as an atheist or agnostic and addressed himself to the relationship between his basic thought and the existence of God. He also developped a «demonstration» for God's existence which we shall examine in the third chapter. This study critically evaluates Gentile's theism; this will include the method of demonstration, his concept of God, and the question of whether he was a theist or not.

In order to treat this problem logically, we must first consi-

[2] These have been published by Sansoni in Florence (Firenze), within the past ten years.

der the fundamental principles of Gentile's system. Therefore, the first chapter will treat of the general characteristics of Gentile's philosophy. It will also deal with Gentile's method (which he calls the «method of immanence») and his reform not only of the realistic but also the idealistic tradition. From these considerations we can move immediately into the place that God and religion hold in Gentile's thought; then we shall move to the question of the reality of God in the third chapter. This third chapter will complement the second chapter, inasmuch as in the latter we see Gentile assuming the existence of God as the objective moment in the dialectical act of the human spirit. However, we should also see how Gentile comes to his God, i.e., following logically the nature of man's knowing process, how Gentile demonstrates God's reality. We shall see that his approach opposes the traditional «a posteriori» and «a priori» types of demonstration because they are founded on Greek transcendence, which Gentile calls the «logic of the abstract.» Gentile's critique of these arguments of the past will form the subject matter of the fourth chapter.

The study will conclude with an attempt to evaluate Gentile's unique contribution to philosophy and to the specific problem of God's reality. We shall consider the influences on his thought and the novel way in which he went beyond those influences. The final chapter will examine the consistence and inconsistency of his thought, the valuable aspects together with the weaker points. We shall attempt to learn to what extent his position is acceptable and whether or not there must be a limit to this acceptance.

We have drawn mainly on the major and relevant works of Gentile rather than on the assorted articles in journals which we feel only repeat the essentials of the doctrine in his books. Not all of Gentile's many works will be used in this study because it is not necessary to use them all. Some of his works deal with pedagogical problems, some with certain individual philosophers and their thought, others deal with political theory or aesthetics. The works which give us the basics of his system must, of course, be seen even if they do not deal with our specific problem. These are the two volumes of his logic, *Sistema di logica,* and also *Teoria generale dello spirito come atto puro,* his work on the act of thinking. I have also drawn heavily on a work on his social philosophy, *Genesi e stuttura della società* (1943), because it was his final effort to communicate his thought. These last two works have been translated into English by H. Wilson Carr and Henry Silton Harris, respectively; however, I have made my own translations of these works. [3] These are, thus far, the only major works of Gentile which have been translated into English. If anyone should care to examine a bibliography of works done on Gentile in the English language, he might consult Volume 9 of the collection *La Vita e il pensiero.* This was compiled by Henry Silton Harris [4] and translated into Italian by N. Terranova.

Since this study is mainly concerned with Gentile's philosophy of God and religion, we shall also draw heavily upon Gentile's own lecture on his religious beliefs, «La mia religione.» This is contained in the latest edition of his work, *Discorsi di religione.* Another major religious work is an earlier one, *Il modernismo e i rapporti fra la religione e filosofia,* first published in 1909. Another work that has been useful for Gentile's criticism of the past as well as an understanding of his intellectual heritage is *La riforma della dialettica hegeliana.* Gentile's own «demonstration» for God's existence (see Chapter Three) has been published in the Sansoni edition of his work *Introduzione alla filosofia.* This work also includes his remarks on the accusations of atheism and agnosticism made against him because of his immanentistic conception of God.

The writings mentioned here are only the basic writings. Many others from his own books, from those of commentators,

[3] Credit is also due to the Rev. Sebastian Matczak, Ph. D., of St. John's University, the Rev. Dante di Girolamo, S.M., and Prof. Amadeo Amendola, Ph. D., of Seton Hall University for their suggestions in the delicate task of translation.

[4] Prof. Harris is presently the chairman of the department of philosophy at Glenmore College, York University, Toronto, Canada.

from articles written in scholary journals and also the Sansoni volumes will be included when deemed pertinent and valuable.

Philosophers who take a realistic position in epistemology are cautioned to be patient with Gentile, since they will readily see his view of the real as antithetical to their own. At a time when so many are prone to claim that «God is dead,» Gentile, who were he here today would claim the opposite, should be heard. It could well be that an understanding of Gentile will, at least, contribute much to an understanding of modern agnosticism.

At this point I would like to express my deepest appreciation to Professor Sebastian A. Matczak of St. John's University for the help and encouragement given me in so many ways. A final word of thanks is also due to my wife, Joyce, who, in spite of other duties managed to spend many hours at the difficult task of typing.

# CHAPTER I

# GENERAL OUTLINE OF GENTILE'S SYSTEM

## 1.- PHILOSOPHY AND PHILOSOPHICAL METHOD ACCORDING TO GENTILE

Gentile's works and thought exhibit a long and careful analysis of the philosophies of the past. His references to other philosophers and their thought is constant and most often critical. His personal philosophical persuasion quickly became antithetical to the positivistic thinking of his time. His tendencies became idealistic as he listened to the neo-hegelian Bertrando Spaventa throught his teacher Donato Jaja. However, these tendencies, which he maintained and intensified throughout a very active life and political career, were not to spare some of the greatest members of the idealistic school from his attacks. Descartes, Berkeley, Kant and Hegel were all found wanting when it came to the development of a true idealistic philosophy. [1]

It would seem that Gentile's principal reason for dissatisfaction with previous philosophers was their inability or unwillingness to free their thinking from certain «presuppositions.» They saw themselves as existents born into a world of other existents. Most accepted the reality of this world without question. They considered themselves as intellectual spectators of this reality around them. They were as finite as anything else in the universe: they came to be, they lived for a while and then passed on. They considered themselves as temporal and did not seriously question their relationship

[1] For Gentile's critique of Kant and Hegel as well as all philosophies of note having «transcendent» presuppositions see Chapters IV and V.

to time, infinity or the eternal. For Gentile a naive common sense realism is not worthy of a philosopher. It places man over against nature, i.e., it sets up an opposition between man the onlooker and knower, and nature, the external reality known. Realism makes the whole of reality an independent object, abstracted from thought. The spirit of man becomes opposed to nature in the realist epistemology.[2] Gentile put the principal blame for this view on Plato and Aristotle as well as all those who followed them. Some have tried to avoid this subject-object opposition but, as we shall see, none succeeded to the satisfaction of Gentile.

### a) *The Method of Immanence.*

In Gentile the «method of immanence» refers to the reform which he believed he had to make of the basic notions of the philosophies of the past. Gentile used this terminology, «method of immanence» in his work on the reform of the hegelian dialectic, *La riforma della dialettica hegeliana.*[3] It was meant to be a critique of the theories of Truth and Transcendence in philosophers from Plato to Hegel. None of these philosophers was able to avoid a theory of duality arising from a conception or reality presupposed and opposed to the act of consciousness, man's act of thinking — whether it was a world of Transcendental Forms, an empirical world or an Absolute. Philosophers were content if they could discover the nature of the universe of matter and mind. The life of the spirit was reduced to abstracting the universal idea from empirical reality or seeing the world as a finite model of the eternal and unchanging Forms. As we shall see later,[4] for Gentile such a

[2] G. Gentile, *La Riforma dell'educazione, Florence,* 1935; also H. S. Harris, *The Social Philosophy of Giovanni Gentile,* Urbana, Illinois, 1960, Introduction; this theme will be considered again from time to time in the study.

[3] G. Gentile, *La riforma della dialettica hegeliana,* Messina, 1913, Chapter X.

[4] Chapter IV.

concept of the spiritual life of man amounts to a materialistic, naturalistic or positivistic philosophy, no matter what its followers might claim. Therefore, the «method of immanence» is intended to rescue philosophers from this one-sided view of man, that is, man as an empirical self, finite, contingent, a mere contemplator and part of the nature which surrounds him. Such a view of man, thought, truth and reality is quite incomplete. It must be completed and the full truth arrived at by a new and more developed view of the immanence-transcendence, subject-object antitheses than has ever been seen before in the history of philosophy. In fact, one's whole concept of the nature of philosophy must change. As we shall see, Gentile's system exhibits definite tendencies toward spiritualistic monism and immanentism.

### b. *The «Act of Thinking as Pure Act.»*

Although it is true that Gentile was very critical of the past, this does not mean that he failed to use his intellectual heritage. His basic doctrine is both a variation and melange of the Cartesian «cogito,» Protagoras' view of man as the «measure of all things, «Berkeley's «esse est percipi» and the dialectic of Fichte. In fact as Roger Holmes well points out, «the dialectic of the spirit is the thread upon which the entire doctrine of actual idealism is strung.» [5] The aristotelean and scholastic epistemologies must now be set aside and the true nature of the human spirit and its activities examined. In his last work Gentile summarized this doctrine which he had long defended:

> ... that realism which even today remains at the foundation of thought, after so many centuries of Christianity, teaching the doctrine of the spirituality of the real and thus the im-

[5] R. Holmes, *The Idealism of Giovanni Gentile,* New York, 1937, p. 29. This work is an examination of the two volumes of the *Sistema di logica* of Gentile.

> possibility of postulating a reality in itself, antecedent to the spirit which knows it and wills it. Realism... is always very naive, because it should be easily seen that whatever is found, invented or constructed by thought, cannot be anything other than thought.[6]

Here we see the monistic and immanentistic tendency which the gentilian philosophy took. Using his own, although not the traditional, concept of Christian teaching and applying it to his philosophical approach to the real, he insisted that Christianity had given him his most basic insight, namely, that the spirit of man is creative of reality as well as of thought. In fact thought must be seen as the very soul of reality.

Two points must be noted here: 1) Gentile is putting emphasis on thought rather than the empirical self. Therefore, one might say that his doctrine is more «logocentric» than «egocentric.» 2) While he realized that many philosophers believed in the thinking power in man, he noticed they often spoke of thought as a type of reality. However, Gentile pointed out that thought is the completed result of thinking, of thinking over and done with. Consequently, a thought is a finished product, a fact, and is not essentially different from the tree which exists independently of us. The intellectualistic view reduces the spirit of man to the order of the natural. As such, it is false.[7]

For Gentile thinking must been as a pure act distinct even from thought which is its object. This pure act is the distinguishing feature of man as opposed to all other things or the earth. This theory of the «act of thinking as pure act,» i.e., an act which is its very essence, was meant to make Gentile's philosophy presuppositionless. Nothing is pre-supposed to the act of thinking. Such a doctrine is meant to solve the dualisms raised by all positivistic and transcendentalist philosophers

[6] G. Gentile, *Genesi e struttura della società,* Firenze, 1946, p. 12 (Tr. mine.)

[7] This view will be considered in greater detail in the following parts of this chapter.

which conceived «reality as a fact independent of any relation to the mind which studies it.» [8] This is not just an idealism but rather an «actual idealism» because the whole of reality itself is reduced to the very *act* of thinking; nor is it a solipcism because other men too have minds or, more precisely, their own acts of thinking; nor is it a panlogism because here is not one great universal Mind but only the thinking of individual men. Gentile's «method» proposes «the internality of all the objects of experience (or the totality of the thinkable) in the activity of the thinking Ego.' [9] For this reason we shall treat the «act of thinking» as opposed to completed thought, although thought is essentially united with the act of thinking; the logic of Aristotle as opposed to Gentile's new «logic of the concrete;» the new viewpoint on the nature of truth; and Gentile's view on the kantian distinction between the «empirical ego» and the «transcendental ego.»

c) *The Distinction between Completed Thought, «Pensiero Pensato,» and the Act of Thinking, «Pensiero Pensante.»*

The section is concerned with Gentile's relationship between thought considered as a completed fact, thought — thought, and the pure activity of thinking which is never completed, expressed by the term «pensiero pensante,» or thought — thinking.

Let it first be noted that what one might call Gentile's epistemology or theory of knowledge is also his metaphysics — his theory of being (essere), his theory of reality. Gentile constantly insisted that one of the great tragedies of scholastic philosophy was that Christians either forgot or misconstrued their Christian heritage and allowed themselves to be

[8] G. GENTILE, *Teoria generale dello spirito*, 6th edition, Firenze, 1959, p. 53. *Theory of Mind as Pure Act*, (tr. by H. Wilson CARR), London, 1922, p. 50.

[9] Patrick ROMANELL, *The Philosophy of Giovanni Gentile, An Inquiry into Gentile's Conception of Experience*, New York, 1938, p. 73.

too greatly influenced by Greek intellectualism. [10] This caused a constant opposing of mind to nature, even the opposition of completed thought (pensiero-pensato) to the act which is thinking (pensiero-pensante). It is this act which is eternal and universal because thinking is a constant becoming. Spaventa, Jaja's and Gentile's intellectual master, pointed out that in the act of thinking, the hegelian distinction between Being and non-Being is overcome because they are only moments of becoming. In this way Spaventa greatly improved the very basis of Hegel's dialectic. Consequently Spaventa could write as follows:

> Thus becoming itself is a beginning that ceases, and a ceasing that begins... I cannot grasp myself as *thinking,* but only as an object of thought, and hence I die as thinking. Yet *in dying* as thinking, I think, and hence I am *born* as thinking. And so on forever. [11]

The subject-object antithesis is overcome in this act of thinking. Consciousness becomes consciousness of the self and what most people consider to be «other» is caught up in this act of self-consciousness. Gentile in his turn tells us:

> Consciousness of another is always consciousnesss of self, because the other is never anything but the Self variously determined in the flow of the unity, in which every conscious being makes himself one with the universe... [12]

Time and time again Gentile warns us that if we think of space and time is the despository of the positive, the real and the concrete, we are thinking of nothing; that the placing of

[10] G. Gentile, *Sistema di logica,* (3d edition), Firenze, 1940, Vol. I, Chapter III.

[11] G. Gentile, *B. Spaventa: Scritti filosofici,* Naples, 1900, pp. 197-200.

[12] G. Gentile, *Il modernismo,* 3d edition, Firenze, 1962, p. 260: «La coscienza dell'altro e sempre coscienza di se, perche l'altro non e mai se non il Se variamente determinate nel flusso dell'unita, in cui ciascun essere cosciente fa un tutto con l'universo...» (Tr. mine.)

reality before thought «untouched by any subjective action» is an «illusion.» What we ordinarily consider as a reality posited as objective and also as a concept conceived by the mind (pensiero pensato) is actually «a reality posited by the subject as such, therefore, absolutely speaking, itself subjective, and non-subjective only relatively to the degree or mode of subjectivity of a reality in all other respects subjective.» [13]

Human life, then, is thought. Subject and object are two terms which are related or tied together in such an unbreakable manner that they form an absolute unity. [14] In his work on the act of knowing Gentile tells us:

> Nature... is only intelligible as the life of the mind, which however it is multiplied remains one... reality is neither spatial nor temporal, because reality is mind and mind is neither in space nor in time. [15]

Leo Lugarini, a recent commentator on Gentile's philosophy, sees this «identification of reality with the act of thinking and the opposition to naturalism as the nucleus of the entire gentilian thought.» [16]

In Gentile's opinion the problem has been that philosophers «failed to attain to the concept of mind as pure act.» [17] Therefore knowledge of reality which is truly philosophic must

[13] G. Gentile, *Teoria generale dello spirito*, p. 116 (Tr. mine). This means that everything which is of nature, i.e., extra-subjective, is interiorized by our mental activity. For Gentile, a thing is objective only in relation to a subject. Man, transcendentally considered, is always considered subjective except for the objective moment which is realized when the world becomes the objective moment of the act of thinking.

[14] G. Gentile, *Discorsi di religione*, (4th edition), Firenze, 1957, pp. 36-37.

[15] *Teoria generale dello spirito*, p. 126 (Tr. mine.)

[16] Leo Lugarini, «Il problema della logica nella filosofia di G. Gentile,» *La vita e il Pensiero*, Vol. VII, p. 145: «L'dentificazione della realta con il pensiero nella concretezza del suo attuarsi, nucleo dell'intera speculazione gentiliana... egli è a oppugnare ogni forma di naturalismo ed in genere di realismo, e si trova quindi condotto ad immanentizzare la realtà all'atto stesso del pensare.» (Partial translation mine.)

[17] *Teoria generale dello spirito*, p. 128. (Tr. mine)

come from the positing act of the knowing subject, i.e., from within the act of thinking itself. The self posits the other and opposes itself to it as a limit — whether this «other» is the world, the State, or God. To oppose an Ego to a non-Ego is what Gentile terms «immediacy.» [18] This opposition, however, is a mere abstraction and a consequence of the aristotelean logic (the Logic of the Abstract). Ego and non-Ego are nothing in such a view. They are something only in their unity, which takes place through mediacy. Consequently, «...their concreteness lies in the mediation of the synthesis whereby the subeject is a subject inasmuch as it is a unity of the two terms; and the same holds for the object. And indeed the subject posits the object, but not as an abstract immediate subject, but as the unity of a synthesis (or a synthetic unity). Which unity does not come after the subject or object, but is first. The act, the synthetic unity a priori, comes first.» [19] An identity of these «opposites» takes place through mediacy, namely, through the human spiritual reality which by a creative synthesis posits the opposed terms and resolves the opposition.

> If, within this synthesis, we distinguished the Self from the non-Ego, the Ego would not be the true Ego nor the non-Ego the true non-Ego. The Ego becomes Ego and the non-Ego becomes non-Ego only trought the synthesis. The synthesis signifies opposition, but it also signifies the identity of the opposites. By positing the non-Self, the Self is put forth as the non-Self. [20]

All syntheses, therefore, arise from the immanent dialectic of the spiritual act. Unity is found in self-consciousness which is «concretely logical,» i.e., self-concept. Gentile points out that here we are not dealing with the abstract dialectic of the knowing spirit but with the real dialectic of the spirit in its practicity. The «pensiero pensante» is eternal and universal

[18] See this chapter, Section e, on Truth.
[19] G. Gentile, *Genesi e struttura della società*, pp. 33-34. (Tr. mine.)
[20] *Ibid.*, p. 34. (Tr. mine.)

since past and future are brought together in it as it thinks them. All things are «assembled and exist within the Ego.» The unity of a man as thinking thought or as transcendental Ego is infinite and absolute and cannot be surpassed. The Ego «thinks of everything in and along with itself.» Subject and object become just two moments within the act of thinking. Gentile tells us that:

> To think means to understand oneself and by understanding oneself, inasmuch as one is distinct from things and from others, to understand this world which surrounds man as diverse from us and similar to us. [21]

There is, however, another and very important aspect of Gentile's thought which must be understood before we can continue. This aspect involves what one might call the unity of thought and action — the moral aspect of thinking itself. In his work which he entitled The Absolute Forms of the Spirit, [22] Gentile tells us that life is action; action and the world cannot be sought outside of consciousness. The world is an eternal flame whose combustion is thought. [23] Practical activity is an activity of the spirit of man. In fact, in his final work, written over thirty years later, Gentile tells us that «one who does not love does not comprehend» and that «Love is... the crowning perfection of knowledge.» [24] Our will tells us of our spirit; the intellect tells us only of nature. In his work on religion Gentile writes:

> The true reality which is that of the spirit, doesn't know, it loves... Therefore the capital importance of faith. Reality, in short, is that reality which the spirit makes to be, and does not presuppose: it is spiritual reality. [25]

[21] *Ibid.*, pp. 44-5. (Tr. mine.)

[22] *Le forme assolute dello spirito* — This little work is a twenty-six thesis summation of Gentile's entire system, written in 1909, and can now be found at the end of his work: *Il modernismo e i rapporti fra religione e filosofia*, (3d edition), Firenze, 1962.

[23] *Il Modernismo*, p. 261. (Tr. mine.)

[24] *Genesi e struttura della società*, p. 47. (Tr. mine.)

[25] *Discorsi di religione*, p. 48: «La realtà vera che è quella dello spirito,

Therefore, in Gentile's actualism (attualismo) everyone is just as responsible for what he thinks as for what he does. Thought must be seen as free and spontaneous. Also, Christianity, in Gentile's view, eliminated the dualism between thinking and willing, between intellectualism and voluntarism, between knowing and loving. Did not St.Paul tell us that knowledge only tends to puff us up, whereas charity edifies? Aristotle made intellectual contemplation the height of spiritual life. The object of this thesis is to bring out the import of consciousness — consciousness as active and creative of its object.[26]

Consequently, the act of thinking is itself a moral act. It reveals the creative freedom which is the essence of our spisitual life. The object of this study is to bring out the import of this belief in relation to God as an existent; therefore, we shall return to this important point later.

d) *The Distinction between the «Logic of the Concrete» and the «Logic of the Abstract.»*

This section of our introduction to the idealism of Gentile («actual idealism») is intended to lead the reader into the very important sections to come — the section on the new, modern interpretation of truth and the section which will deal with the rapport between the true authentic self and the world. Many commentators have correctly pointed out that in order to understand Gentile's philosophy, one must see how Gentile understands other philosophies and then how he transcends them. This includes even those philosophies which have usually been considered immanentistic and idealistic. In

non si conosce, sì ama... Quindi l'importanza capitale della fede. La realtà insomma e quella realtà che lo spirito fa essere, e non presuppone. È realtà spirituale.» (Tr. mine.) (In his translation of *Genesis and Structure of Society*, Harris translates «realtà spirituale» as «conscious freedom,» which I think is valid.)

[26] *Sistema di Logica*, Vol. I, p. 34.

Chapter IV we shall see his critique of these philosophies in some detail but at this point some mention must be made if we are to understand his approach to reality and especially to the problem of the reality of God.

If any single philosopher must stand accused of leading others down the wrong path of philosophical method I would submit Aristotle as Gentile's «villain.» The «method of transcendence,» be it that of Aristotle or of «Greek intellectualism» in general has led philosophers astray in their search for the nature of Truth and Reality. Much of the two volumes of the *Sistema di logica* (System of Logic as a Theory of Knowing» [27] is an attempt to distinguish the aristotelean Logic, which Gentile calls the «Logic of the Abstract,» from his own which he calls the «Logic of the Concrete.»

By now it should be clear that in man, concretely considered, knowing and being (conoscere e essere) are identical. Therefore we can understand why Gentile makes no real distinction between logic and metaphysics. For actualism, logic is not just a special branch of philosophy or the «instrument» of philosophy, but rather it is philosophy itself. The term «il logo» or logos may have various meanings. *Logos* provides the truth value for judgments; as a term it fulfills the function of that in relation to which thinking is ultimately either true or false; it deals with reality in its intelligibility. [28]

The Logic of Aristotle took a naturalistic attitude and presupposed a fixed, stable world. A knowledge of it could only lead to the formation of static concepts. Ideas were compared to things. Positive science built its methodological approach to the study of reality on this basis. Many philosophers used the aristotelean syllogistic process [29] and thought according to aristotelean first principles: the principles of identity, noncontradiction and excluded middle. Metaphysical arguments for God and the immortal soul were founded on these principles, considered as first principles, both of thought and of

[27] The full title of this work by Gentile is: *Sistema di logica come teoria del conoscere*, Firenze, 1940.

[28] R. HOLMES, *op. cit.*, p. 34.

[29] The aristotelean syllogism is a «petitio principii» according to Gentile.

Being. Not even Kant and Hegel were able to rid themselves of the «intellectualistic residua». However, as Romanell points out, Gentile did not want to destroy Aristotle's Logic but wanted an «inveramento,» i.e., a rectification. The «Logic of the Abstract» attempts to put us in immediate contact with the diversity of beings and so opens us up to the epistemological problems of finite selves.[30]

The gentilian «Logic of the Concrete» can find these aristotelean categories in the epistemological setting of a philosophy of transcendence, i.e., a philosophy which believes that the penetration of the real demands knowledge of entities which are outside the act of thinking, entities which pre-exist or transcend the act of thinking itself. Gentile's logic is not a spectator's worship of simple facts contemplated by a substantial mind. The «Logic of the Concrete» sees mind and spirit not as a «fact» but as an «act.» In this setting reality becomes the very thought itself by which we think it. The subject-object dualism must fall to their synthesis in the dialectical act of thinking. Reality becomes an activity of the very spiritual act which creates it.[31]. Will and Intellect are synthesized in this act. Logic, therefore, becomes the very process of knowledge itself. Knowledge becomes self-constituted. In conclusion, let us hear from Gentile himself:

> The modern age is precisely the slow, gradual conquest of subjectivism; the slow, gradual identification of being and thought, of truth and man; it is the founding of the kingdom of man which was celebrated for centuries, the establishing of a true humanism.[32]

[30] P. Romanell, *op.cit.*, pp. 84-5. This is Romanell's doctoral dissertation written expressly on the subject matter of this first chapter.

[31] The «concrete logos» might be understood as the activity generated by the will.

[32] G. Gentile, *La riforme della dialettica hegeliana*, pp. 122-3: «L'étà moderna è appunto la conquista lenta, graduale del soggettivismo; la lenta graduale immedesimazione dell'essere e del pensiero, della verità e dell'uomo: è la fondazione, celebrata nei secoli, del *regnum hominis*, l'istaurazione dell'umanesimo vero.» (Tr. mine.)

e) *Truth.*

One might begin this very important section by clarifying one point: Gentile did not deny that things other than himself existed. His active life, as well as many passages in his works, gives ample proof that he was neither a practical nor a theoretical solipcist. Gentile was merely trying to communicate his belief that the naturalistic attitude was not worthy of the philosopher; that one could never accomplish the aim of philosophy — the penetration of the life of the spirit which is man — if he started with the presuppositions of Greek intellectualism. To philosophize one must grasp the immanent activity of thinking itself:

> To think means to understand oneself and by understanding oneself, inasmuch as one is distinct from things and from others, to understand this world which surrounds man as diverse from us and similar to us. And thinking lies in understandding that Absolute, God, at the core of things and man, that is, at the core of itself, whereby everything is sustained and kept in harmony. To understand all of this is what every man does even if he does not have a clear concept of this immanent act of creating whence everything he thinks penetrates his very being, and thus he truly succeeds in thinking.[33]

We see then that Gentile would grant that Nature, the realm of the existing, when contraposed to thought as thought's limit, is represented as just the totality of individuals coexisting in space and time.

Gentile did not admit that which philosophers for years had considered to be the philosophic enterprise, namely, the knowledge and classification of the natural world. Philoso-

[33] G. GENTILE, *Genesi e struttura della società*, pp. 44-45: Pensare significa intendere sé stesso; e per intendere sé stesso, in quanto egli si distingue dalle cose e dagli altri, intendere questo mondo diverso da noi e simile a noi, onde l'uomo e circondata; e in fondo alle cose e agli uomini, ossia in fondo a sé medesimo intendere quell'Assoluto onde tutto si regge e s'accorda: Dio. Intender tutto questo è quel che fa ogni uomo anche se non abbia un chiaro concetto di questo suo fare immanente onde compenetra di se tutto quello che pensa, e così riesce in verità a pensare.» (Tr. mine.)

phers wanted to bring the natural world inside their minds and know it as it is. They believed that they possessed their great goal of «Truth» when there was an «adequatio» or correspondence between reality (external) and the way they judged this reality to be in their minds; the judgment could be considered to be a «pensiero pensato.» I think that Gentile could understand and forgive the Greeks for submitting to such an «illusion» but was surprised and disappointed that the Christian tradition should have believed such a theory. First of all, Gentile believed that such a relationship between material reality and mind materialized the mind. There can be no adequate representation in the mind which could be caused by the spatial, multiple or extended (one might note the influence of Berkeley here). An object can only be immanent to the act of thinking in virtue of the act of the subject itself. The mind's spatializing activity generates multiplicity. The spatial is such thanks to the activity of the transcendental ego (which we shall soon consider). Secondly, the Christian philosophers missed the main point of the Christian message, namely, that nature and the flesh must be opposed to a truer world or reality. This is not the world that a man is born into but rather it is one which he creates of his own will. This is the kingdom of the spirit. Nature is always internal to the restless activity or dialectic of the intellect and will which synthesizes itself in the progress and life of the spirit. «God's will be done» is the Christian imperium, and Gentile points out that the Christian must accept and accomplish it.

What is important for man is not the world which he finds but the world, or even the God, which he makes and leaves after him. True knowledge is the love which makes our world, whereas simple knowing only presupposes it. The Christian, told by St. Paul that he is nothing without charity,[34] must see consciousness as active and creative of its object.[36] That Aristotle thought contemplation to be the height of the spiritual

[34] St. Paul, *Corinthians*, I, 8, 14.

[35] *Sistema di logica*, Vol. I, pp. 33-4: «Il mondo pertanto non è più quello che c'è, ma quello che ci dev'essere; non quello che troviamo, ma quello che lasceremo: quello che nasce in quanto con l'energia del nostro spirito lo facciamo nascere... Il vero conoscere adunque è amore... Alla conoscen-

life Gentile could understand. However, the Christians seemed to have been much more enamoured of Plato and Aristotle than of their own heritage.[36]

We, therefore, should not think in terms of a psychology which divides mind or thinking into powers or faculties and call the intellect the faculty of truth which is immediately aware of the multiplicity of the world. Mind is non-multiple. Its unity is infinite. Its unity implies its infinity.[37] For Gentile truth must share this absolute character of mind and therefore «otherness» must be overcome. The object must enter into the life of the subject — not immediately as an object of the intellectual faculty, but rather as what Gentile calls «mediately.» Immediacy fixes the object and makes it an abstraction; the «logo concreto» does not do this. It does not make truth immanent to the subject and at the same time hold that it transcends the act of knowing — in fact such a «truth» is not even a knowable reality.[38] Gentile asserts:

> Immediacy has this significance: that the subject introduces no truth of its own, by means of its own processes, extraneous to the transcendent nature of truth...[39]

The Logos is born in the act of knowing. Truth does not come from the world or from an act of thinking that has al-

za intellectualistica contemplativa, che era ad Aristotele la cima più alta dell'ascensione spirituale, sottentra una conoscenza nuova, attiva, operosa, creatrice del suo soggetto, cioè di se medesima nel suo spirituale valore.»

36 Gentile is referring to the words of St. Augustine: «Noli foras exire, in te ipsum redi, in interiore homine habitat veritas,» (*De Vera Rel*, 39, 72), namely, that truth lies within man, not outside of him. Gentile cites this often, e.g., see his *Discorsi di religione*, p. 117.

37 *Teoria dello spirito*, p. 30.

38 *Discorsi di religione*, pp. 66-7: «Questa alterità dell'oggetto e pertanto la vita del soggetto, se questa si deve concepire dialetticamente, come svoglimento e non come un presupposto immediato, a modo della vecchia psicologia metafisica... Fissare questo oggetto, nella sua oggettivita, e fissare un astratto...».

39 *Sistema di logica*, Vol. I, p. 63: «Immediatezza che ha questo significato: che il soggetto non introduca nella verità nulla di suo, mediante suoi processi, estranei alla nature trascendente della verità.» (Tr. mine.)

ready taken place. Coming to the truth is a «mediate» process and this is accomplished in the self-consciousness of one's thinking. To say that «man is mortal» is a judgment of the logic of the abstract. One would do better to say: «I think man is mortal,» since this is a mediation between «I think» and «man is mortal.» The truth relation lies in the «I think.» I am also conscious or aware of my freedom to make this act of thinking. The subject as free gives this assertion its truth value.[40] When we think of something, we must think of it as being true and the true is one and absolute, not relative. It is not subject to the multiplicity and spatiality of temporal things. It transcends them and says what must be thought about them. Truth is eternal and it implies the eternal act in which it is revealed.[41]

In the «Logic of the Concrete» the subject-object duality is overcome because in the knowing and speaking of things, they are within us. «Otherness» becomes just a «stage of our mind» through which we pass without stopping. The subjective and objective become two moments of the pure act of knowing. The subject becomes subject and object in their unity. The unity does not exclude the duality, but it does not consider it abstractly, only concretely, i.e., in its identity.[42] Truth, therefore, is not external to the actual process of discovering it. For truth is also my truth, and thus concrete truth; an act of my very being. It is a truth which we must love, because generated by our own thinking.[43]

[40] Cf. R. Holmes, *op. cit.*, pp. 40-47.

[41] *Teoria dello spirito*, p. 137: «L'eternità del vero importa l'eternità del pensiero in cui il vero si manifesta ... sentire in sè la verità, non può esser altro che sentire in sè l'eterno, o sentirsi partecipi dell'eterno...».

[42] *Sistema di logica*, Vol. I, pp. 146-7: «Dentro infatti allo stesso soggetto, dialetticamente concepito come posiziòne di sè, risorge nell'atto del puro conoscere la differenza dei due momenti, soggetiva e oggettiva... Il soggetto, insomma, del puro conoscero è soggetto ed oggetto nella loro unità... L'unità... non esclude, la dualità: dualità non intesa essa stessa astrattamente, ma concepita nella dialettica della sua vita concreta... Assoluto opposto, ma non meno identico che opposto.»

[43] *Ibid.*, Vol. II, pp. 317-19: «La verità che dobbiamo amore ... e quella verità che dev'essere generata dal seno del nostro stesso pensiero... La verità veramente pensata è verità nostra, e percio *concreta*.»

## 2.- THE DISTINCTION BETWEEN THE «EMPIRICAL EGO» AND THE «TRANSCENDENTAL EGO»

The gentilian distinction between the Empirical and Transcendental Egos is in a certain sense the culmination of his method of immanence and the doctrine of actual idealism. The distinction is a part of Gentile's «reform» of German idealism as it is found in Fichte and Kant, although Gentile rarely refers to Fichte.[44]

As has already been mentioned, the philosopher worthy of the name, the philosopher who is a Christian and would benefit by his heritage as well as the modern spirit, must renounce the naturalistic as well as the transcendent attitude. One must realize that although actual idealism is ontologically logocentric, it recognizes the empirical situation of each man, of man's history, his environment, the State, etc. As Holmes points out: «... actual idealism brings in all significances, poetic, religious and scientific; and insists that each play its role in the whole. But it is only the whole that it has been willing to call philosophical...»[45] The empirical self is the self which thinks in terms of dualisms: subject-object, body-mind, God-the world, etc. It is the self whose logic is the logic of the abstract. Its world of reality is reached by a mind which is substantial rather than a constructive process or development. Man and his mind, considered as empirical, exist in space and in time; they know only with difficulty.

As far as Gentile is concerned, this empirical aspect of man is valid but incomplete and non-philosophical. Realism has its place, but it does not give us the entire picture of reality. As we shall see later, not even the kantian idealism is entirely free from realistic presuppositions as well as an opposition between the Self and the «thing-in-itself» to which speculative thinking cannot attain. The real «Self» of man is the «Self»

[44] For a good exposition of this distinction and the Fichtean dialectic see F. Copleston, *A History of Philosophy*, Vol. VII, Part I, Garden City, N.Y., 1965, pp. 50-120.

[45] R. Holmes, *op. cit.*, pp. 244-245.

devoid of all presuppositions — the «transcendental Self.» This is the «thinking Ego.» Herein we find man's absoluteness, his eternal and infinite aspect as opposed to the temporal and finite. Multiplicity is overcome in the unity of the act of thinking of the transcendental Self. Space and time are caught up in this unity. As Romanell explains it: «The actual is the 'eternal present.' A distinction is made between a temporal present and an eternal present. The former is an element of time; the latter is the 'principle' or intelligibility of time.» [46] Time and eternity, the infinite and the finite are overcome and resolved. Without this immanent relation between the two «selves» each is falsely conceived. The empirical ego simply *knows* the world, the transcendental ego *creates* the world. The transcendental ego overcomes immediateness as well as the distinction between the intellect and the will. Knowing and willing become but two moments of the spirit. The world becomes as man, in his absolute self, sees it and determines it to be. Gentile writes as follows:

> Thinking in its very actuality as the self-creating of reality, is knowing inasmuch as it is willing and willing inasmuch as knowing. [47]

The transcendental self, therefore, is the ground of consciousness and creative freedom, a self-positing absolute self. Copleston states in his exposition of Fichte's theory that: «... the absolute ego posits within itself a finite ego and a finite non-ego as reciprocally limiting and determining one another.» [48] The absolute or pure ego stands «beneath» the

[46] P. Romanell, *op. cit.*, pp. 77-78.

[47] *Discorsi di religione*, p. 55: «L'idealismo attuale è transcendentale perchè il suo pensare, come verità del pensato, è lo stesso Io puro kantiano, ma concepito senza transazioni con le esigenze dell'ingenuo empirismo realistico... Questo idealismo, se è anche esso anti-intellettualistico, come idealismo cristiano, non è volontaristico; ha superato cosi l'uno come l'altro di questi punti di vista antagonistici... Il pensare, nella sua attualità, come autocreazione della realtà assoluta, è conoscere in quanto volere, volere in quanto conoscere.» (Partial translation mine.)

[48] F. Copleston, *op. cit.*, p. 66.

individual finite self. It is the self which cannot be turned into an object of consciousness (ergo, a pure act of thinking). It transcends objectification, since «every act of objectification presupposes the pure ego. And for this reason it is called the transcendental ego» and «it manifests itself in the activity of objectification.» [49] I submit that although this is being said of Fichte, it may also be said, to a great extent, of the absolute self of Gentile. [50]

Therefore, in order to treat reality philosophically, we must release ourselves from our empirical, finite and individual status by a process (svoglimento) of self-consciousness (autocoscienza). Babois correctly interprets Gentile to mean that:

> ... this material individuality, in a sense extrinsic, must be transcended by man in his spiritualizing act, in order to construct his spiritual individuality, completely which should be the way in which he participates in the absolute «Self»... Man should create this spiritual personality within himself as completely interior apart from his material individuality... [51]

Spirit, immanence and subjectivity must be distinguished from nature, but will and intellect, creativity and knowledge must not be separated. Man must be seen in his real «character» which belongs properly to his will. [52] Gentile says:

> And as long as the will, which is in time, is considered in its temporality, it cannot appear to be endowed with character. [Its organic unity and completeness.] Character is more

[49] *Ibid.*, pp. 60-61.

[50] However, as we shall see later in Chapter 5, for Fichte the objectification of the non-ego is performed unconsciously, while for Gentile it is performed consciously.

[51] Eduard Babois, «Genesis and Structure of Society,» *Revue Philosophique de Louvain* (1955), pp. 442-443: «...cette individualité matérielle, extrinsèque en un sens, l'homme doit la transcender en la spiritualisant, pour constituer ainsi son individualité spirituelle, tout intérieure, c'est-à-dire sa personalité morale, qui doit-être sa manière à lui de participer au 'Moi' absolu... Cette personalité spirituelle, tout intérieure, l'homme doit la créer en lui, à partir de son individualité matérielle...» (Tr. mine.)

[52] *Genesi e struttura della società*, p. 29.

> in a will which contains time but is not in time: in a Self which is not an empirical Self, to use Kant's terminology, which we know from experience, but in a transcendental Self which knows everything that can be contained in experience.[53]

We shall see the application of this distinction to the knowledge of God's existence in the second and third chapters. However, it should be evident by now that one must understand Gentile's philosophical approach in order to treat the problem of God in a competent manner. One must oppose the method of immanence, the logic of the concrete, the act of thinking itself and the transcendental ego to the method of transcendence, the logic of the abstract, thinking as completed and the empirical ego. These distinctions are of importance for determining the place of God in Gentile's philosophy. Depending upon which side one takes, one must either deal with the traditional philosophical dualisms or transcend them. The varied works of Giovanni Gentile are concerned with the application of the method of actual idealism (i.e., reality as immanent to the pure act of thinking) to these dualisms as they are wont to appear in the various branches of philosophical speculation. We are mainly concerned with the dualism of God and the human mind, or God and man. To some extent this is a religious question, i.e., what is the relation of the human spirit to the Divinity in whose image this spirit is created? For this reason I think we should consider certain aspects of Gentile's religious philosophy. Even a brief treatment will open up for us the specific problem of God and give the reader a deeper insight into Gentile's conception of philosophy and the application of actual idealism to the problem of God.

[53] *Ibid.*, p. 30; (tr. mine); see also: *Teoria generale dello spirito*, pp. 6-8: «Io empirico ed lo trascendentale.»

# CHAPTER II

# THE PLACE OF GOD IN GENTILE'S SYSTEM

## 1.- THE FREQUENT REFERENCE TO GOD

Gentile's concern with God permeates all the years of his philosophical activity. In 1898 he mentioned God in his writings on Marxism. From 1903 to 1909 he was concerned with the religious education of youth in the primary and secondary schools. In 1909 he clearly posited God as the object of religion and the objective moment of the dialectic. He also developed his theory on mysticism. From 1909 to 1920 he was concerned with the attempt of Catholicism to deal with the heresy of Modernism. He concluded that religion and philosophy were two irreducible forms of the human spirit. In 1926 he made a public expression of his faith in God. However, in 1934 all of Gentile's works were condemned by the Holy Office and placed on the Index of Forbidden Books. In 1939 he returned to his thought of 1909 and taught that the font of religion is the moment of objectivity of the human spirit. Man experiences a «mystical moment» which is immediate union with God. In his lecture «La mia religione» given in 1943, there is evidence of a sensitivity over the condemnation of his works. He states that he is trying to be «frank,» «explicit,» and as «clear as possible,» and expresses the hope that others will not substitute their words or thoughts for his. He also affirmed his Catholocism since birth. In his final work, *Genesi e struttura della società,* 1943, he dealt with the relationship between God and religion, and God and the State.

Moreover, the name of God is frequently mentioned throughout almost all of Gentile's writings and lectures. Three of his major works were specifically addressed to religious questions such as the problem of God, the God-man relationship, religion, and religion's concomitant phenomenon which is mysticism. These works are *Il modernismo e i rapporti fra religione e filosofia* (1909), *Il problema della scolastica* (1913), and the *Discorsi di religione* (1920). In this last work God is spoken of at least sixty times. God is also mentioned frequently in some works not directly related to the problem of God; thus, God is mentioned at least forty-five times in the *Teoria generale dello spirito come atto puro,* and in the *Sistema di logica,* and also in the *Genesi a struttura della società* over forty times.

In spite of these frequent references to God it should be noted that Gentile's main philosophic interest or purpose is not the study of God as transcendent but the understanding of man. This understanding involves two aspects: man as an abstract-finite being and man as concrete being. Man in his abstract-finite aspect is temporal and limited; in his concrete aspect he is timeless and infinite. The infinite aspect of man is revealed in man's self-consciousness or in his pure act of thinking. As a consequence these aspects render the transcendent God of traditional philosophy unauthentic and in a sense unreal. These aspects are treated mainly in the *Teoria generale dello spirito come atto puro* (1916) and the *Sistema di logica* (1917). These are his main and basic works.

Therefore, the problem of God as absolutely transcendent to the rest of reality is not the primary concern of Gentile's system. As we shall soon see, Gentile did not tolerate a real separation or dualistic interpretation of the God-world relationship because this would be inconsistent with his basic method of immanence. Yet God explains man just as man explains God. For this reason Gentile must frequently refer to God.

## 2.- GOD AND RELIGION

### a. *Religion as a Moment in the Life of the Spirit.*

Gentile considered himself to be a religious man because he believed in the life of the spirit and in man as a spiritual reality. Therefore, as we saw in the Introduction, he considered himself to be a Christian, since Christianity is a religion of the spirit. [1] The search of the life of the spirit which penetrates the whole of reality is an important aspect of philosophy for Gentile. In this search philosophy discovers itself.

In one of his earliest works [2] Gentile spoke of «the absolute forms of the spirit.» These «forms» follow the essential moments of the spirit: the position of the subject, the position of the object and the position of their synthesis. Corresponding to these three moments of the spirit are three absolute forms of the spirit: art, religion and philosophy. These three are distinct but nonetheless bound together by the very same relationship as the spirit's three moments. Genile states: «Art is consciousness of subject, religion is consciousness of object, philosophy the consciousness of the synthesis of subject and object.» [3] Gentile calls both subject and object «contradictory» when considered in themselves. Each must integrate with the other. This integration or resolution of the one into the other is philosophy.

In his last work, *Genesi e struttura della società*, written over thirty years later, Gentile returned to a consideration of this dialectic. He tells us:

[1] As we saw in the Introduction, he considered himself to be even a Catholic Christian. In the article «La mia religione» contained in the *Discorsi di religione*, p. 124, he declares: «Ripeto dunque la mia professione di fede... io sono cristiano. Sono cristiano perché credo nella religione dello spirito... io sono cattolico. E non da oggi; sia anche questo ben chiaro. Cattolico a rigore, sono del giugno del 1875, ossia da quando sono al mundo.»

[2] «Le forme assolute dello spirito,» first written in 1909 and republished in *Il modernismo*, pp. 259-265.

[3] *Ibid.*, p. 264: «L'arte è la coscienza del soggetto, la religione la coscienza dell'oggetto, la filosofia la coscienza della sintesi del soggetto e oggetto.»

> Religion just as art is the non-real which becomes real in the self-synthesis of the concrete life of the spirit; in which there is neither abstract subject nor abstract object but only the one face to face with the other, each remaining what it is in its non-reality, in opposition with the other: each one inseparably bound in the original and necessary bond of self-consciousness or thought.[4]

This text becomes clearer if we keep in mind that by «self-synthesis» Gentile understood philosophy. Thus religion becomes concrete in philosophy which is self-consciousness and synthesis of subject and object. Therefore, the subjective and objective moments are only logically distinguishable. Each must be integrated and resolved in the final form which is philosophy. Herein we find truth, the full actuality of the spirit. There is no pure religion because there is no pure or abstract object. As a moment of the spirit it is transcendental and therefore must be caught up with the others in the eternal reality of the act of thinking.[5] As transcendental they are not to be considered as existing alone but only together, as realizing themselves together in the immanent union of the spirit.

b. *Religion as the Antithesis of Art.*

Before entering the subject matter of this section, a word is in order with regard to art as a moment of the spirit. It would be more precise to say that art is a moment in the life of the philosopher whose life is a continuous dialectical act of his spirit and a self-awareness of it.

Art is consciousness of subject. In this center of activity

[4] *Genesi e struttura della società,* p. 132: «La religione come l'arte è l'inattuale che si attualiza nell'autosintesi della concreta vita dello spirito; in cui non è né astratto soggetto né astratto oggetto; ma l'uno di fronte all'altro, restando ciascuno qual è nella sua inattualità, in opposizione con l'altro: l'uno e l'altro legati inscindibilmente nel nesso originario e necessario dell'autocoscienza o pensiero. (Tr. mine.)

[5] G. Gentile, *Il modernismo,* p. 262: «Questi momenti si possono dire percio nel linguaggio kantiano, *transcendentali*: ossia transcendenti l'atto reale eterno del pensiero, a cui sono realmente immanenti, solo dal punto di vista dell'analisi di esso reale eterno del pensiero.»

which is the subject, the world is individualized.[6] For the poet and the writer the world around them exists as they see it. Reality for them is that which is known as they know it. The subject, as such, gives form to the world and to philosophy; it does not give content. Yet each philosopher studies the same content as the artist but more comprehensively. Therefore, philosophy and each philosopher must be understood in terms of subjectivity, although such an aspect is incomplete.

The complete view of the philosophical life must include the antithetical moment in the life of the spirit, the objective. The antithesis of art is religion, i.e., the consciousness of object as mere object. Actually it is not possible that religion can exist in itself as a pure form or in a pure state of objectivity. In reality it can never escape from its relationship to the religious subject. Pure object is unknown, yet, one might say that it is unknown in a certain way — as unknown. Every object is determined, since it is the object of a determined subject.[7]

At this point in his exposition of the «absolute forms of the spirit» Gentile turns from the art-religion or subject-object antithesis to a consideration of the object of religion. Presuming that everyone is agreed that the object of religion is God, he tells us:

> The object of religion, as the object of art, is not absolute from the philosophic point of view, but absolute from the religious or artistic point of view. The God of the poet is his Genius; the God of the saint is just the Unknown. On the one hand we have the immediacy of light; on the other, the immediacy of darkness and mystery; on the one hand the exaltation of the subject, on the other his self-prostration and self-annihilation.[8]

[6] *Ibid.*, p. 265: «L'arte è coscienza del soggetto... Il soggetto, questo centro della coscienza stessa, e però del mondo, puntualizza in sè e individualizza il mondo, costringendolo nell'attimo del proprio atto.»

[7] *Ibid.*, p. 269.

[8] *Ibid.*, p. 269: «L'oggetto della religione, come l'oggetto dell'arte, non e

One should keep in mind that objectivity and objective being, whether given in terms of God or the State, always presented some difficulty for Gentile. In order to realize oneself as a person, one must transcend this objectivity. Man the person, the knower, face to face with the Unknown or God, represents the central religious problem. Let us now consider this central problem briefly.

c. *Mysticism as the Essence of Religion.*

In his *Discorsi di religione* Gentile tells us that «the essence of religion is mysticism.» [9] The mystical is an attitude which one may take in his approach to God. I submit that Gentile did not consider it to be the philosophical or authentic attitude. In the mystical attitude, which is a phase of the life of the spirit, God must be considered as unknown, absolutely other than the self. One's own autonomous self must be annihilated before God. The mystic must want to lose his selfhood in the life of God. [10] The mystic sees God as everything and man as nothing. God is unknown, a God of mystery, an abstract object known by man in the manner of immediacy and yet unknown. God and religion, therefore, become the dominion of religious faith alone. [11]

In his *Teoria dello spirito come atto puro* Gentile compares the idealistic and mystical aproaches to God. In this work Gentile points out that the grave defect of mysticism lies in

assoluto dal punto di vista filosofico, ma assoluto dal punto di vista religioso o artistico. Il Dio del poeta e il suo Genio; il Dio del santo e appunto l'Ignoto. Da una parte: l'immediatezza della luce; dall'altra, l'immediatezza della tenebre e del mistero; da una parte l'esaltazione del soggetto, dall'altra il suo prosternarsi e annullarsi.» (Tr. mine.)

[9] *Discorsi di religione*, p. 58.

[10] *Ibid.*, p. 58: Gentile cites St. Paul, *Phillip.*, 1, 23: «Desiderium habeo dissolvi et esse cum Christo;» and *Gal.*, 2, 20: «Vivo autem, jam non ego vivit vero in me Christus.»

[11] *Ibid.*, pp. 140-141: «Anch'io, sì, ho sempre parlato di ignoto e di mistero, come dominio della fede religiosa... Dio tutto, e l'uomo niente: è il motto del mistico, lo spirito più logicamente religioso.»

its rejection of the distinctions in this «dark night of the soul.» Finite things and even our concrete personality disappear within the «womb of the infinite.» This leads to a weakening of human endeavour; it tends to discourage scientific research and rational knowledge. [12]

Idealism, on the other hand, resolves all distinctions. The finite and the infinite are each recognized both in their difference and in their identity. [13] In spite of appearances mysticism is essentially intellectualistic. It posits opposites and eliminates one — man. It therefore has its epistemological basis in the pre-Christian philosophy of ancient Greece. Gentile's idealism is anti-intellectualistc and therefore rejects mysticism as does the more mature form of Christianity. [14]

However, as Gentile sees it, the mystics ridicule the intellectualistic theories because such theories vainly attempt union with the Absolute through knowledge (conoscenza), whereas the mystics feel that union with the Absolute must come through love, transformation of the self, a creative process. The spirit of man must be immersed in the Absolute through this process. Both intellectualism and mysticism make God external to the subject, something knowable waiting to be known. The «proper characteristic» of intellectualism lies in this accord. Each presupposes its object as already realized before the knowing process begins. Therefore, mysticism cannot escape from this intellectualistic tendency. Gentile says of mysticism:

> ... and in spite of all its efforts it does not succeed in discerning in the spirit as will (sentiment, love), because will is liberty, self-constitution; and this is not possible where activity is not absolute... [15]

[12] *Teoria dello spirito*, pp. 254-255.

[13] *Ibid.*, pp. 255-256: «L'idealismo risolve tutte le distinzione, ma non le cancella come il misticismo, e afferma il finito non meno risolutamente che l'infinito, la differenza non meno che l'identità.»

[14] *Ibid.*, p. 256. Here Gentile probably means augustinian Christianity.

[15] *Ibid.*, p. 257: «... e non riesce, malgrado tutti i suoi sforzi, a concepire lo spirito come volontà (sentimento, amore), perchè volontà è libertà, autoctisi; e questa non è possibile dove l'attività non è assolute...» (Tr. mine.)

For two reasons, then, the mystical approach to God and religion insofar as it encourages this approach, is non-authentic: 1) it is based on an intellectualistic presupposition; 2) it necessitates the negation or abnegation of the self; it eliminates the act of self-constitution which is an authentic act of the spirit. As such mysticism must be denied a role in an idealistic philosophy which places the highest value on the concrete Self, the person considered as spirit and presuppositionless in its act of knowing.[16]

## 3.- THE REALITY OF GOD IN GENTILE

In this section I shall set forth some further notions on Gentile's philosophy of religion. His last works show greater development than the 1909 systematic presentation of his *philosophy. This section will draw mainly from* his *Discorsi di religione,* his *Teoria generale dello spirito,* and his *Genesi e struttura della società,* in which his notion of religion is more developed and which I feel has been justly called his «spiritual testament.»[17]

### a. *The Problem of Transcendence.*

Gentile seems to be well aware of the doctrine of transcendence in the Judaeo-Christian theology and philosophy. Gentile held that treating of God in His Transcendency is the function and tendency of religion. God is represented as immediately Infinite. He is unknown, ineffable and hidden from man. Gentile believed that God is presented as extraneous to man and the world and must be conceived that way and that it is of the very nature of mystical theologies to negate the character of the person. The negation of subjectivity in favor

[16] See R. Holmes, *The Idealism of Giovanni Gentile,* p. 125. Mysticism is an immediate awareness of God, not a mediate process.

[17] Armando Carlini, in his «Postilla» to «Dall'immanenza alla trascendenza dell'atto in se,» *G. Gentile: La Vita e il Pensiero,* Vol. VIII, p. 45.

of objectivity and the emphasis placed upon transcendence was believed to be one of the causes of agnosticism and atheism in his time.[18]

As Gentile saw it, Christian philosophy (that of some of the Fathers and that of the Middle Ages) did not adhere to the true (Gentile's) interpretation of the Christian revelation given by St. Augustine.[19] Christian dogma, under the influence of neo-platonic thought, had made God as well as the world transcendent to man. According to Gentile the ancient Greek naturalism joined to the scholastic notion of God as First Uncaused Cause, Necessary Being, the one Being whose essence is identical with His act of existing,[20] has created an insurmountable obstacle to our knowledge and true appreciation of human knowing and liberty. Such a viewpoint makes it impossible to know God and therefore religions tend to develop myths which give fantastic forms and names to the divinity.[21]

Such philosophy created a chasm between the finite and contingent creation on the one hand and the Infinite and Necessary God-Creator on the other. It created the problem of crossing the chasm by acts of knowledge and love. Modern philosophy generally feels that as long as these presupposi-

[18] *Discorsi di religione*, pp. 62-63: «Consequenza della posizione religiosa del divino come negazione assoluta della soggettività è l'agnosticismo, che è il carattere negativo di tutte le teologie mistiche... Il *Deus absconditus* è la divinità di tutte le religione: l'Innominabile, l'Ineffabile, che non si conosce se non immediatemente... La ragione dell'agnosticismo religioso è questa svalutazione o annientamento del soggetto...»

[19] Cf. supra, p. 14.

[20] St. Thomas AQUINAS, *Summa Theol.*, I, 2, 3. (Tr. by English Dominican Fathers), New York, 1914.

[21] *Discorsi di religione*, pp. 60-61; also *La riforma della dialettica hegeliana*, p. 123: «Religiosamente, l'opposizione platonica della verità alla mente, la separazione assoluto del divino dall'umano è negata la prima volta dal Cristianesimo, nella travagliosa elaborazione del domma dell'uomo-Dio. Ma filosoficamente la teologia cristiana rimane impigliata nella rete del platonismo e aristotelismo, e quando la filosofia moderna proseguì l'opera, che essa aveva iniziata, di intrinsecare il divino con l'umano, le si volse contro nemica...».

tions are tolerated, man must be united with God by religious faith alone.

This problem of course reduces to the problem of «otherness as such.» If we are to investigate the notion of God as other than the world we must first examine the epistemological foundations for the distinctions Gentile makes. Objectivity must be «resolved in the real activity of the subject who knows it.» [22]

If we apply the «method of immanence» to the problem of God's transcendence we will have to consider the question in a new light — devoid of presuppositions. Gentile found fault with religions because they tended to set God off and apart from man and then told man to reach out for God, to search for Him in the cosmos or on the altar. Because of this presupposition some men have despaired of ever finding God and have become agnostics. Armando Carlini, a modern commentator on Gentile, may well be correct when he says:

> In reality, that absolute immanentism was only a polemical attitude against an erroneous concept of transcendence... the transcendence which was not rooted in the very womb of immanence... [23]

In other words, a transcendence which seemed to be absolute takes no account of the knowing activity of the believer or the man in his state of prayer or adoration.

In a very real sense God is «other» than finite, empirical man. He is «the absolute foundation of things and men... the power that maintains all in harmony...» [24] However, it is the task of the modern philosopher to point out that this is not the only manner in which God should be known. Nor does it suffice to say that God is immanent to the world by His

[22] *Teoria dello spirito,* p. 15.

[23] A. Carlini, *op. cit.,* pp. 40-41: «In realtà, quell'assoluto immanentismo era soltanto un attegiamento polemico contro un concetto errato della transcendenza... la transcendenza che non era radicata nel seno stesso dell'immanenza...» (Tr. mine.)

[24] Cf. *supra,* p. 13.

essence and power.[25] This presence would still be external to man. In this notion of immanence God is still externalized and naturalized, and therefore an abstraction, the pure object of our immediate knowledge. The answer to this problem lies in the true appreciation of the immanent-transcendent relation as given in actual idealism. As Gentile explains it:

> Strictly speaking, there cannot be another outside of us if we know of it and speak of it. To know is to identify, to overcome otherness as such. Otherness is simply a stage across which we have to pass if we are to obey the immanent nature of our spirit. We pass but we do not stop. When we find ourselves before this spiritual being as before something different from ourselves, from which we should distinguish ourselves, and something which we presuppose as existing before our own birth... it is a sign that we are not as yet truly in the presence of this being as spiritual being, and we do not perceive its true spirituality.[26]

The general meaning of Gentile's thought indicates that any «spiritual reality,» including God, which is transcendent in the traditional sense of the word, is materialized or spiritually annihilated.

The Christian religion and philosophy unfortunately held a doctrine of the transcendent reality of God and thought that in so doing they had spoken the complete truth and honored God at the same time. Christians had held that God was «il presupposto» of the world and of man in the world. The scholastics reduced God to the manner of existing of the Greek

[25] St. Thomas Aquinas, *op. cit.*, I, 8, 3.

[26] *Teoria dello spirito*, pp. 16-17: «*Altri*, oltre di noi, non ci puo essere, parlando a rigore, se noi lo conosciamo, e ne parliamo. Conoscere è identificare, superare l'alterità come tale. L'*altro* è semplicemente una tappa attraverso la quale dobbiamo passare, se dobbiamo obbedire alla natura immanente del nostro spirito. Passare, non fermarci. Quando ci troviamo dinanzi a quest'essere spirituale come a qualche cosa di diverso da noi, da cui ci dobbiamo distinguere, e che presupponiamo anteriore alla nostra nascità... è segno che noi non siamo ancora propriamente in presenza di quest'essere come essere spirituale, e non ne scorgiamo propriamente la spiritualità.» (Tr. mine.)

Forms, denied Him a true spiritual reality and placed an insurmountable obstacle between Him and human understanding. [27] It is no wonder that God must remain unknown, a «Deus Absconditus» for those Christians who have come under the Greek influence. Divine Transcendence and mysticism become intimately connected because the traditional doctrine of transcendence demands the mystical approach to God together with its unfortunate consequence of the negation of man — «the being of God is our non-being.» [28]

In Gentile's opinion most Christians seem to have forgotten their own doctrine that man is made in the «image and likeness of God,» that man is the «imago Dei.» They have forgotten that it can only be the pure act of thinking, self-consciousness that makes a man to be like God and yet not be God himself. God is immanent, but not in the traditional sense. The latter does not overcome transcendence. God in the cosmos simply -- this view of God retains His «otherness.» Atheism, agnosticism and Greek naturalism can only be overcome by a truly Christian notion of immanence. God must become a moment of the dialectic of each man's thinking act. This involves an immanent «creation» of God by man, which is a function of each man's spiritual activity. This mode of God's reality will be considered in greater detail in the next chapter.

b. *God as Subject and Object.*

«Actual idealism» has as one of its prime goals the elimination of dualisms. Since philosophers have always posited the subject-object dualism as one of the most important because of tis relationship to the problem of Truth, Gentile dealt with it extensively. For Gentile the whole problem was a false one because it was based upon presuppositions found in Greek philosophy. The whole notion of object as opposed to subject was a conception of Aristotle's abstract logic.

The logic of the concrete tells us that human life is most

[27] *Discorsi di religione,* p. 49.

[28] *Ibid.,* p. 60.

evidently manifested through thinking and in this thinking the subject and object are two terms bound together in an unbreakable and absolute unity. Because of this gentilian theory everything which the ordinary person would call external is invested with the individual person's subjectivity, caught up in each man's act of self-consciousness whenever the object is thought of. Gentile, according to Holmes,

> ... is not concerned with the existence of other selves because he takes the position that we can have no necessary or universal knowledge of the existence of such transcendent entities. The real for him is his own act of thinking, and other selves partake of reality only insofar as they are entertained in thinking. Hence the problem of other selves does not arise. [29]

The problem of subject-object opposition is a problem of man empirically considered. However, it is far more important for Gentile that man be transcendentally considered. Only then can reality become the totality of the thinkable and any philosophic knowledge of reality must be endowed with the subjectivity of thinking.

Religion has made God an object of adoration. The true philosopher cannot tolerate this abstract position. A concrete position must be taken which would not exclude the abstract but would rather contain it. Philosophy will contain religion and in so doing God will become present in the concrete life of the spirit. In this way God becomes something more than a mere «object of adoration» which is the abstract position. God will become not merely an object but the unity of subject and object; this will be His concrete existence as far as men are concerned. [30]

Again we see that the «method of immanence» demands that this opposition be discarded by the authentic philosopher. In religion alone God stands off from me, He is «outside» of

[29] R. Holmes, *op. cit.*, p. 138.

[30] *Discorsi di religione*, p. 69: «Non sarà il mero oggetto; ma, come unità del soggetto e dell'oggetto, come vero, attuoso soggetto, deve essere puro oggetto;» see also: *Introduzione alla filosofia*, (2nd. ed.), Firenze, 1952, pp. 200-201.

me and I cannot be truly, i.e., mediately, united with Him. This type of God and this view of God has no value, no place in philosophical speculation. Philosophy recognizes only true immanence which is self-consciousness and its own act. Even if we posit God as an object we immediately immanentize Him in the very act which makes us His «image.» The objectivity of God is overcome in this thought which is constantly thinking on itself, constantly aware of itself and therefore divine, universal and eternal. Subjectivity and its proponent modern philosophy overcome objectivity and the older positive, empirical philosophies. Concomitantly, atheism and agnosticism are also defeated and made to seem absurd.

This then is one way in which the Divine is immanent to His creation. The section on Jesus Christ will consider the other way.

c. *Elimination of the Distinction between the Finite and the Infinite.*

«Actual idealism» also rejects the time-honored distinction between the finite world and the infinite or unlimited God, the Absolute.[31] According to Gentile the distinction is valid on the empirical and abstract level of experience only. However, this takes away its philosophical validity, for philosophy, according to Gentile, «is the consciousness of the synthesis of subject and object.» Gentile continues:

> The subject which is object resolves the individuality of pure subject in the universality of pure object, freedom within the law, the *finite* in the *infinite,* the relative in the absolute.[32]

Infinity, then, is the attribute of an object which has no conditions which might modify its essence. Such has been the traditional concept of theism. God was the Creator of the

[31] This problem will be treated in detail in the next chapter.

[32] *Il modernismo,* p. 271: «Il soggetto che e oggetto risolve la individualita del puro soggetto nella universalita del puro oggetto, l'arbitrio nella legge, il *finito* nell'*infinito,* il relativo nell'assoluto.» (Tr. mine.)

world. His essence and existence being identical, He needed nothing other than Himself. This made God independent of the world while the finite world remained dependent upon Him. God was, and is still considered by many theists, the necessary and unlimited Being, while man and the world must always be contingent and finite.

How is this unknown God, this God with wordly limitations, to be known by man? How is man ever to be united with Him? The human intellect as a knowing instrument is supposed to be merely finite. The result of a purely intellectual investigation can only be scepticism as regards God's existence and nature. On the other hand Gentile does not seem to want to reduce God to the status of «logical being,» a product of his own or someone else's thought. The Infinite must be brought within the finite or otherwise our contact with God can be only religious or mystical. This will not suffice; nor will Gentile risk the belief that man is the creator of God. As we shall see in the next chapter, man «creates» God only in a certain restricted sense.

The non-intellectual interpretation of mind in actual idealism holds the key to the problem. The faculty psychology is one of dead abstractions for Gentile. Mind is non-multiple. The new interpretation of mind says that it is infinite. It is infinite because of its unity: «Its unity implies its infinity.» [33] This means that it cannot be limited by other realities and still keep its own reality. All reality can be brought within the «pensiero pensante.» Gentile holds that:

> ... whatever effort is made to think or imagine things or consciousnesses other than our own consciousness, these things or consciousnesses always remain within it, precisely because posited by us, although posited as external. Whatever is outside us is always within. [34]

The human mind and man himself, if transcendentally and concretely considered, is neither in space nor in time. The life

[33] *Teoria generale dello spirito,* pp. 30-31.
[34] *Ibid.,* p. 32.

of man is the life of the spirit and this because of man's power of self-consciousness, because of his thinking. Thinking is philosophy and philosophy can be only idealism.[35] Our own thinking knows no limit: the spirit «cannot refer itself to an object which is external to it.»[36] The mind's world is within it. Spirit never just is, but is becoming without end, therefore, infinite. It is a false and nonphilosophical attitude which places any thing or concept before or beyond it. The act of thinking is one, not multiple. Multiplicity, space and time are resolved within it. The doctrine of an Absolute, Infinite God, unknown and forever unknowable, this God of religion, is the object of Gentile's attack. Being, or God as Infinite, must only be a moment of a dialectical or synthetic process. On the other hand, the spirit of man as concretized in the act of thinking goes beyond this process. It has a moral or creative aspect as well. This further aspect of the spirit will be seen in the next chapter.

## 4. JESUS CHRIST AND HIS ROLE

Since it was Gentile's intention to eliminate the older dualism between God and man, we have considered the application of the «method of immanence» to the problem and seen his demand for a synthesis of the two. However, being a Catholic Christian, suo modo, he recognized the presence of Jesus in the world and His uniqueness. His treatment of Jesus' presence is interesting because it seems to raise a new problem for him.

As we have seen, Gentile wanted to eliminate the older notion of divine transcendence and make God not only immanent to creation on the cosmic level but immanent to man himself. This was the most important aspect of immanence, the truly philosophical. True immanence should mean self-

[35] *Discorsi di religione,* p. 57: «La vita umana è vita spirituale. Ma vivere spiritualmente è pensare; pensare è filosofare; filosofare è idealismo; e l'idealismo dev'essere idealismo attuale.»

[36] *Teoria generale dello spirito,* p. 33.

transcendence, i.e., «autocoszienza» and its act.[37] Therefore, God becomes immanent to our own act of self-awareness. Gentile realized that this doctrine had caused Catholic priests to preach against him because of his humanization of God by giving divine attributes to human thinking. However Gentile defends himself by pointing out that it is God Who, in a way, had humanized Himself. Although Gentile is not perfectly clear in this matter, he seems to be saying that this humanization took place on two levels or in two ways in our history. Excluding the notion of the State as a divine institution, the Divine entered the world in the form of Jesus Christ as well as in the form of the human spirit.

Is Jesus really the divine, transcendent God of religion? One must seriously doubt that Gentile held himself to be an expert in the theology of the Incarnation. If he were an expert, one would think he would have been more consistent in his remarks on the role Jesus played in human history, as well as His true nature. In one place in his works he speaks of Jesus as a teacher taught by God and ranks Him alongside Buddha and St. Francis of Assisi.[38] This, of course, would give Jesus no claim to divinity. In another place he states that Jesus was «made to arise and ascend into heaven,» and he describes this event as «a popular myth.»[39] Myth or not, traditional theology held that Jesus' resurrection from the dead was due to His own power and that by this miracle He conclusively demonstrated His oneness with God, i.e., His true Divinity. However, Gentile is not at all clear on this point. Jesus is given some authority in one of the last pages of Gentile's last work where Gentile states: «Did not even Jesus say that in order to be saved one must be ready to lose one's soul?»[40] In this section of his book we have an instruction from Jesus or immortal life, yet this does not establish that His authority to teach does not come from God rather than from Himself, inasmuch as He too is God.

[37] A. Carlini, *op. cit.*, p. 45.
[38] *Genesi e struttura della società*, p. 146.
[39] *Ibid.*, p. 145.
[40] *Ibid.*, p. 156.

At this point it would seem that the humanization and immanentization of God must take place in some other manner alone. In the same section of *Genesi e struttura della società* where Gentile speaks of death and immortality, it is pointed out that God is humanized in the sense that God is discovered within man and that in a certain way man creates Him. Man, of course, is like God because man, concretely considered, is spirit. In his lecture «La mia religione» Gentile said the same thing:

> The man who finds God in himself and in a certain way therefore creates him, is not the natural man, but the man who is spirit, entered already into the kingdom of the spirit, whence he is man but also God.[41]

However, man is not God, for on the very same page of the above lecture Gentile tells us that man and God are really distinct, although not separate. They are two abstract terms of a synthesis which is created by the human spirit, by self-consciousness, by the act of thinking which is also a moral act, i.e., an act of the will.[42]

Now, what is to be said of Jesus? In spite of what we have seen written in Gentile's last work, *Genesi e struttura della società,* he seems to hold that Jesus was divine.[43] Nevertheless, he is somewhat vague on this point. In his discourse on his religion he stated that man does not create God nor does man create Jesus.

Therefore, unless all this has some deeper meaning, it would seem that man is divine because the divine spark is

[41] G. Gentile, «La mia religione,» in *Discorsi di religione,* p. 140: «L'uomo che scopre in se Dio, e in certo modo quindi lo crea, non è l'uomo naturale, ma l'uomo che è spirito, entrato già nel regno dello spirito, ond'è uomo ma è anche Dio.» (Tr. mine.)

[42] *Ibid.*, p. 140: «L'uomo e Dio sono certamente distinti; ma non sono separati sé non come termini astratti dalla vivente realtà che è sintesi. Sintesi di Dio che si fa uomo che la grazia adegua a Dio, facendo dalla sua la divina volontà (fiat voluntas tua).»

[43] *Ibid.,* p. 140: «E il Dio che si umanizza è il Cristo; e chi, mercè sua, partecipa della sua divina natura.»

manifested in the human spirit, manifested by human liberty. In addition to this, the Divine was in the world in the person of Jesus. However, although Gentile does not explicitly point it out, Jesus was a historical personage who, as man, had a temporal duration in a certain period of time. In the terminology of «actual idealism» (or perhaps better «actualistic idealism»), He was external to the act of thinking and therefore perhaps not worthy of philosophical consideration. Even in His Eucharistic Presence Jesus would be an external object, adored on an altar and kept inside a tabernacle under accidental forms.

It would seem, then, that in the person of Jesus, the infinite, Absolute and Transcendent God entered the world of time and space. Nevertheless, divine or not, Jesus can be considered only as an aspect of the religious moment in the dialectic of the absolute forms of the spirit.

Thus the question of Gentile's theism may be raised. However, before attempting to examine this theism, let us conclude this chapter with a brief consideration of Gentile's theory of the State. This is relevant to our chapter because of the fact that the State took on the aspect of a «religion» in Gentile's system.

## 5.- FASCISM AS A SECULAR RELIGION

As we have seen, religion is the objective moment in the dialectic of the spirit; it is one of the «Absolute Forms» of the spirit. We have seen that the traditional conception of Christianity can easily lead to the negation of man by God. Actual idealism, therefore, felt it necessary to try to salvage the dignity and importance of man without turning to a humanistic atheism.

One may easily see an analogy between this attitude toward the man-God problem and another very important problem in Gentile's work, the man-State problem. Gentile became intimately involved with the new (1922) Italian State when Mussolini asked him to write a philosophical doctrine for the

Fascist regime. [44] Gentile realized that one very important task would be to preserve the individuality of each person as manifested in his acts of liberty; self-determination was the mark of the spirit of man in the world. The individual must not be subsumed within the State just as he must not be subsumed within the hegelian Absolute. The spirit of man as opposed to mechanistic nature gives man his great dignity in the universe. It makes him like God: «Man, in truth, is free... inasmuch as he interiorly realizes himself as conscious of himself, as a thinking being... creator of himself.» [45] The State, like God, stands outside each man and precedes him in existence. Each man is in danger of suffering the negation or annihilation of his life and freedom by the force of this external power. Like the laws of God, the laws of the State are a presupposition of his moral life. Gentile realized the danger of absolute power vested in one or a few men. Nevertheless, the State had a definite will toward its citizens, and since God reveals His own Will to men throughout history, the State is very probably the organ for the manifestation of this Divine Will. One can easily see the importance which must be tendered to the ruler of such a State. Gentile held that even violence can be a holy or divinely-willed violence. [46] God can be immanent to His creation through the State and its leader.

The State is the universal common aspect of the will; it seeks to achieve unity among the people by realizing the will of the people. [47] Fascism was the party of the Italian State. It had its canons and its cult of martyrs. However, the State and its laws are only an abstract moment in the ethical life. The positive law of the State and the moral law which comes

[44] See Wm. A. Smith, *Twentieth Century Fascism,* New York, 1965, pp. 23-25 and 31-33.

[45] *Discorsi di religione,* p. 35: «L'uomo, in verità, e libero ... inquanto si realizza interiorimente come coscienza di sé, come essere pensante... creatrice di se stessa.» (Tr. mine.)

[46] Gentile was criticized for sanctioning the use of blackjacks by Fascist «squadristi» during street fights.

[47] *Genesi e struttura della società,* p. 88; see also Herbert Schneider, *The Making of the Fascist State,* New York, 1928.

from the human spirit itself must be transcended in a concrete act of the will. The synthesis will realize human liberty with order. In a discussion of the State and religion Gentile said:

> In the dialectic of the Will, God is the moment of law, the moment of past decision. The rigidity of the law has something of the ineluctable necessity of the divine nature. [48]

In a certain way, the State and its law takes on the aspect of a religious institution — at least in the case of the Fascist State.

For Gentile, Fascism is a living idea, a direction of thought, an inspiration and a tendency in which spirits encounter each other. «In this nucleus there is unity and faith.» [49] Gentile agreed with Giuseppe Mazzini that the Italian State possessed a special holiness. [50] The Fascist State, according to Gentile, was not the agnostic State of the old liberal order which immediately preceeded the Fascist rise to power. The Fascist State is an ethical state, a concrete will, a moral activity, i.e., an activity which wills what it should will according to an ideal — the national consciousness. The ethical state is spiritual, a system which is will, thinking, «the story of a people told in the living fire of an actual and living consciousness.» [51]

In his book *Che cosa e il fascismo*? Gentile entitled one of the sections: «Fascism is a Religion.» In this section he tells us that while Fascism is a political party and a doctrine it is also a «total conception of life.» Like a true catholic who carries a full sense of his religious committment throughout his whole life the fascist must match the catholic's acts of prayer and meditation, be it in the parliament, at the office, in the family, in his writings or in his conversations. The fasc-

48 *Genesis and Structure of Society*, p. 150; *Genesi e struttura della società*, p. 89: «Nella volontà Dio è il voluto, la legge. La quale, nella sua rigidezza ha la necessità inderogabile del divino.»

49 G. Gentile, *Che cosa e il fascismo* ? Firenze, 1925, p. 12: «In quel nucleo è l'unità e la fede.»

50 *Ibid.*, p. 33.

51 *Ibid.*, p. 36: «...storia di un populo raccolta nel fuoco vivo di una coscienza attuale a viva.» (Tr. mine.)

ist must give the people a sense of their glorious past. The good of Fascist Italy must become the object or goal of the efforts of all the Italians. Like the good catholics they should make day to day sacrifices and if necessary die for their ideals, ideals which must be connected with the good of the State. The will of the people and the will of the State must be resolved in a synthetic unity. If this is accomplished it must follow that Italy, past, present and future, would be the object of Italian respect and sacrifice.[52]

A difficulty which can be found in all of this is that, for all practical purposes, the Fascist State does take on many of the aspects of a religion which puts a demand upon the loyalty of its followers. Nevertheless, Gentile retains his concept of traditional religion and states that a true «secularism» could accept a religious body within the State and transcend it. The State and its citizens should promote the welfare of traditional religion but strive to resolve the immediacy of religious dogma through the critical mediation of the self-concept (reflective thought). Gentile continues:

> But God, even when He is unrecognized or ignored, is always present in the depths of our hearts; He goads and torments and disturbs us as long as He remains undiscovered or unconfessed. And He exists immediately, always there before our eyes, in the iron logic of the system of nature with all its necessary laws.[53]

These statements seem to open up the possibility of three religions: the traditional, Fascism and even actual idealism, whose God exists within our thinking act. Is the traditional concept of religion to be subsumed within the concept of the

[52] *Ibid.*, pp. 38-39.

[53] *Genesis and Structure of Society*, p. 150; *Genesi e struttura della società*, p. 89: «Ma Dio, anche ignorato e disconosciuto, è sempre li nel fondo del nostro cuore; e ci punge, ci agita, ci turba finche non sia stato scoperto e confessato. Ed è li, sempre immediato, innanzi ai nostri occhi nella sua ferrea logica di essere necessario nel sistema di tutte le sue necessarie determinazioni.»

State or that of the thinking subject? Is this Gentile's true thought when he says:

> As an ethical institution in the full sense, the State returns again from objective divinity to the infinite divine spark in the heart of the subject, the point at which the universe has its center.[54]

This problem together with that of the nature of Gentile's God will be considered at greater length in the final chapter.

[54] *Ibid.*, p. 150; *Genesi e struttura della società*, p. 89: «E come piena moralità ricorre dal Dio oggetto di Dio infinito che è alla radice del soggetto, punto in cui s'incentra in tutto.»

# CHAPTER III

## THE DEMONSTRATION OF GOD'S EXISTENCE IN GENTILE'S SYSTEM

Having considered the relationship between God and man within the religious situation, let us now see how man makes his personal approach to God within the method and system of actualistic idealism. This chapter will deal with the positive approach of immanence. The next chapter will examine his criticisms of the demonstrations offered by many of the philosophers who preceeded him. However, before we begin, a word of warning is in order. Gentile's argument for God's existence is not based on the transcendent dualism of knowing subject and object known but rather places the emphasis on immanence. Subject and object become one thanks to the presence of the transcendental ego. Each man is considered to be a subjective moment in the whole of reality and Gentile's arguments for God's existence involve an act of self-consciousness within which and by which objective reality is known and loved. In a certain sense each man «creates» or «makes» his God instead of using aristotelean reasoning to prove He exists apart from us. Each man in a sense «makes» God to be rather than discovering Him through His manifestations in the world. Therefore, one should not expect a proof similar to those of traditional metaphysics.

### 1.- PRELIMINARY FACTORS LEADING TO GOD'S EXISTENCE

It should be recalled that when treating of the nature of the «pensiero pensante» in the first chapter,[1] we alluded to

[1] Cf. *supra*, p. 5.

the fact that the true Self of each man does not consist in a «pure act of knowing» alone, i.e., it is not purely cognitive. Thus, Gentile considers man as spirit but only when he is philosophically and therefore authentically treated. In other words, man is manifested in his ethical tendencies and this in turn includes his freedom from mechanistic causes. Gentile often mentions this characteristic of man throughout his major works. In his *Teoria generale dello spirito,* «mind is freedom» [2]; in his *Genesi e struttura della società,* he tells us that our duty is «to will the Good» and «the Good is the activity of the spirit.» [3] The liberty and freedom of man which is due to his spiritual nature is a theme which runs throughout this book. [4] He emphasizes the point that the spirit of man is more than a cognitive faculty. Man's spirit is dynamic. It makes the truth to be what it is. It makes our knowledge possess the epistemic properties of truth and certitude. [5] Thinking therefore has a moral aspect. We are as responsible for what we think as we are for what we do. While he says that our thinking, which is the center of our ethical life, «appears to us as a kind of feeling,» he develops this thought even more:

> The «thinking» that constitutes the ethical category is *more* than mere feeling; it is self-conception; the concrete Ego, a synthesis of Ego and non-Ego. It is self-synthesis. We speak of moral feelings and a moral sense only because the root of this self-conception is in the immediate awareness called «feeling.» This root is what gives thought its life and universal value; from it the development of self-consciousness must necessarily begin; and in it lies the spontaneity that is the starting point of liberty. [6]

[2] *Teoria generale dello spirito,* p. 37: «Lo spirito è libertà; ma è anche, e appunto perciò, legge, che esso distingue de sè come superiore alla sua propria attività.»

[3] *Genesi e struttura della società,* p. 51.

[4] This is because Gentile is trying to resolve the individual-State antithesis into a synthesis of liberty with law and order.

[5] Gentile often cites Spinoza's dictum: «Verum norma sui et falsi.»

[6] *Genesis and Structure of Society,* pp. 113-114. In a footnote to this

The life of the spirit, then, is not mere knowing nor mere feeling (immediate awareness). The life of the spirit is basically the self-synthesis of Ego and non-Ego, which is self-consciousness — but a self-consciousness of my unity with others. It is knowing and feeling. This unity is due to the fact that man is a spirit. Man is aware of himself as the synthesizing or unifying activity of subject and object by his spirit — the concrete Ego. Its unifying activity and self-consciousness is not only a thinking activity, it is also a making or a doing.

Gentile puts this in another way when he points out that philosophers and even St. Paul put great emphasis on the role of love in the activity of the human spirit. However, they could not free themselves sufficiently from the Greek «intellectualistic residua» to comprehend that knowing and loving must not be separated in the life of the spirit.[7] This love of which Gentile is speaking, however, is not a love from afar, it is not a contemplative love. It is a creative love — a love for my truth, my language, my will and for my very being: «The truth which we should love is that truth which we must generate in the very womb of our act of thinking itself.»[8] To know and to love or to do are one and the same spiritual act. The thinking life and the moral life are one. In his major work on religion, *Discorsi di religione,* Gentile applies his philosophical method to his theory of love. After attacking the platonic-aristotelean tradition as absurd because of its treatment of external reality as a presupposition to be contemplated and thought about, he states:

statement H. S. Harris sees evidence of a «change of aspect» in Gentile's idealism. I would agree that it is a further penetration of the «life of the spirit» from his *Sistema di logica* (1917) to his *Philosophy of Art,* published in 1931. It appears not only in the books I have mentioned but also in the *Discorsi di religione.* See also *Genesi e struttura della società,* pp. 48-49.

[7] Gentile criticized Immanuel Kant and St. Paul for this oversight. See Chapter V.

[8] *Sistema di logica,* Vol. 2, p. 318: «La verità che dobbiamo amare... è quella verità che dev'essere generato dal seno del nostro stesso pensiero.»

> The reality which is that of the spirit, doesn't know, it loves; it is not before us, a spectacle which we can enjoy, even if only passively: it is before us only if we make it to be so. Hence the capital importance of faith. Reality then is that reality which the spirit makes to be, and does not presuppose. It is spiritual reality.[9]

Aside from the problem of a possible spiritual monism being presented here (which we shall consider later), the unity of knowing and willing is affirmed. The aspect of spirit as unifying factor is emphasized and thinking or cognitive relation seems to be entirely dismissed. In the light of his entire system, this «bracketing» of the cognitive is undoubtedly for the purpose of emphasizing the volitive or creative aspect of thought, the union of love and understanding.[10]

From this theory Gentile draws his argument for God's existence. However before applying this theory to the problem of God's existence, we should briefly examine a concomitant concept of the human spirit, the concept of man as «self-constitution.» This notion must be seen first in order to analyze the notion of the human will as creator of reality.

In his last work, *Genesi e struttura della società,* Gentile identified will or volition with «self-constitution» (autoctisi).[11] Gentile tells us that the product of man's will is not something

[9] *Discorsi di religione,* p. 48: «La realtà vera che è quella dello spirito, non si conosce, si ama: non è innanzi a noi, spettacolo che noi si possa, anche passivamente, godere; è innanzi a noi soltanto se noi facciamo che ci sia. Quindi l'importanza capitale della fede. La realtà che lo spirito fa essere, e non presuppone. È realtà spirituale.» (Tr. mine.) See also p. 51: «... lo spirito non ha presupposti, e percio è creatore.»

[10] *Ibid.,* p. 55: «Il pensare, nella sua attualità, come âutocreazione della realtà assoluta è conoscere in quanto volere, volere in quanto conoscere.»

[11] In a footnote on p. 73 of *Genesis and Structure of Society,* H. S. Harris explains the origin of the word «autoctisi» which is not really Italian: «The word *autoctisi* was coined by Spaventa from the Greek «*ktisis,*» which the Church Fathers used to describe the creation of the world out of nothing. It means literally 'self-founding !' Gentile often speaks of the spirit as creating itself, and *autoctisi* is his technical name for this self-creation. But perhaps because it is such a fundamental conception in his thought, it is hard to define precisely what is meant by it.» Cf. *supra,* p. 53.

external to the will but is always within it and identified with it. The will is spiritual activity and so, like thought, presupposes nothing to itself.» In Gentile's concept of self-constitution «knowing coincides with willing» and art, religion, economics and philosophy flow from this self-constitution — which also means «moral responsibility or freedom.» [12]

We could now pose the question relevant to our investigation: Does the human spirit, considered as both thinking and willing, create God? Is God a creation, a creature, and man His creator? Gentile himself admits that he has often been accused of professing the affirmative answer to these questions. Gentile seems to have given various impressions, e.g., that God is only what I mean by the word God; that God is a product of the thought of each man and exists only within it. As we shall see in the final chapter, these notions have led to the accusation of atheism, an accusation which Gentile vigorously denied. [13]

Nevertheless, Gentile is somewhat to blame for bringing this criticism upon himself. Besides using the dubious and perhaps vague distinction between the empirical and transcendental Egos to explain his theory, he had occasionally made statements which would seem to corroborate the above accusations. In one of his earliest and major works he stated:

> We may say of spiritual reality what the great Christian writers have said of God. Whoever seeks Him shall find Him. But to find spiritual reality one must be willing to put his whole being into the search, as though he would satisfy the deepest need of his own life. *The God you find is the God whom in seeking you make to be.* Therefore faith is a virtue and supposes love. In this lies the folly of the atheistic demand that the existence of God should be proved to him without his being relieved of his atheism. [14]

[12] *Ibid.*, pp. 74-75.

[13] H. Schneider in his *Making of the Fascist State*, New York, 1928, p. 252, cites a fascist named J. Evola, who, in the journal *Critica Fascisto* (Oct., 1926), said that the fascists themselves are «the creators of God.» Schneider thought this to be «slightly exaggerated rhetoric.»

[14] *Teoria dello spirito*, pp. 27-28. Cf. *infra*, p.69, footnote.

Gentile goes on to say that philosophers (meaning those of a non-augustinian orientation) have wasted their time in trying to show atheist «spirit in nature» and that the psalmist was correct when he said that only the «fool» could ever say in his heart: «There is no God.» One must believe and love and understanding will follow. One must feel the truth within himself and in so doing, he feels the eternal and participates in the eternal.[15]

In another early work, *Il modernismo,* Gentile, having mentioned that consciousness creates authority, states that Galleati-Scotti had the merit of resuming the thought of Gioberti's *Catholic Reform* (*Riforma Cattolica*) in which Gioberti had said that «the authentic man *creates* for himself his own Church, his own God, his own cult, his own dogma... I am free as God himself creates the world.»[16]

Bianca Bianchi, an Italian commentator on Gentile's philosophy of God and religion pointed out the proximity between the thought of Gentile and Laberthonniere, who had observed that God comes within our soul through love; that we can intellectually demonstrate God's existence but once, whereas we can love Him throughout our entire life: that love is a demonstration, a «realization of God»[17]

Within the spirit of man there is realized the unity of Truth and Good Will, knowledge and love.

This theme of the sprit of man as creative will be seen again in the sections to come. However, it might be remembered that if the «method of immanence» demands the non-consideration of objective presuppositions, then reality for each man

[15] *Ibid.,* p. 137.

[16] *Il modernismo,* p. 67: «L'uomo a rigore crea a se stesso la sua Chiesa, il suo Dio, il suo culto, il suo dogma... Io sono libero come Dio stesso crea il mondo.» (Tr. mine.)

[17] B. BIANCHI, *Il problema religioso in Giovanni Gentile,* Firenze, 1940, p. 77: «Dio, osserva il Laberthonnière, è una realtà che si raggiunge con l'amore in seno all'anima nostra. Dimostrare Dio si potrebbe una volta tanto, amarlo non si può se non sempre, tutta la vita. Ma l'amore è una dimostrazione eterna... perchè è una realizzazione di Dio.» One might note here that the theme of the «amor Dei intellectualis» of SPINOZA'S *Ethics* runs throughout Gentile's works.

must somehow give form and matter to whatever the realist would say we think about. Let us now consider this creative aspect of the Self with respect to God.

## 2.- THE TRANSCENDENTAL EGO'S ACTIVITY

Throughout his life Giovanni Gentile was accused of atheism and agnosticism because of his approach to God. At first glance Gentile's view would seem to make God a creature of man, or man the creator of God. If human thinking is productive and creative of its object how can it be otherwise? Roger Holmes's commentary on the *Sistema di logica* contributes to this impression by its contention that not only is God given significance by our thinking but that neither God nor nature is independent of our act of thinking. [18] One must read Holmes, and of course Gentile, very carefully in order to understand exactly what is meant by these statements on the creativity of thinking. At times Gentile seems depressed in spirit because he could not make his intellectual adversaries understand his position.

Gentile even went so far as to attempt his own demonstration of the existence of God. [19] Since this demonstration entails a careful analysis of the notions of transcendental, transcendent and empirical realities, it would be wise to recall a few points which were treated in the first chapter. Keep in mind that for Gentile most of philosophy and all positive science view man as a finite being, both in mind and body. He occupies space in time. Nature and God are transcendent to him and come within him only conceptually, i.e., as concepts or thought-thought. This is man empirically and abstractly considered. His attempts to demonstrate God's existence and to know God were doomed to failure or at least to a resulting agnostic attitude. [20] This was due to the presupposi-

[18] R. Holmes, *The Idealism of Giovanni Gentile*, p. 19.

[19] This demonstration can now be found in Gentile's *Introduzione alla filosofia*, pp. 188-208.

[20] This is a reference to the «via negationis» or «via remotionis» used by scholastic philosophers and will be considered in Chapter IV.

tion that a finite mind was all that man could utilize in order to know the infinite God; that all this finite intellect could use was the physical world in order to come to a knowledge of spirit. In addition to this Gentile criticized the use of the principles of non-contradiction and identity, the indispensable condition of thought for neo-platonists and neo-aristoteleans. For Gentile these were principles of the logic of the abstract, a logic which functioned only in the empirical world, the world of nature, which was transcendent to the empirical self. [21] The physical world can be only an object of thought for an intellect, and therefore rigid, petrified and immutable. The empirical intellect thinks on a world which is antecedent to it. Therefore, using the logic of the abstract, man must move from the finite to the infinite using the physical to arrive at the spiritual. The result, according to Gentile, has been continued controversy and incertitude, agnosticism and atheism.

In the actualistic philosophy it is not man empirically considered who «creates» the world (or God). It is man considered as spirit that «creates» and thus overcomes objectivity and otherness as such. An «other» is a limit and spirit knows no limitations. Spirit is creative and it is everything or it is nothing. Man, transcendentally considered, i.e., considered as spirit, is an eternal process of self-differentiation and self-unification. He is not just particular and individual but universal and infinite as well. He is a «dynamic unity or dialectic of the finite and the infinite, the particular and the universal... the infinite is not immediately in the finite, but mediately» because in the dialectic of the act of thinking by which the subject looks into his own inwardness and realizes himself «the finite and the particular is universalized and made infinite and the universal and the infinite become incarnate in the finite». [22] The transcendental ego has to be creative because thinking is never objectified. Even the objective moment is the

[21] These principles as seen by Gentile will be examined in greater detail in the next chapter.

[22] Ugo Spirito, «Giovanni Gentile," *Enciclopedia Filosofica*, II, pp. 638-639.

result of an act of self-positing. The subject as creative is all the true dialectic can allow for.[23]

The implication of this view of man as it relates to the nature of God was not lost on Gentile. Just as we do not distinguish the faculties of intellect and will in God so, Gentile held, we should not distinguish these faculties in man because of the unity of spirit. Therefore, thought and will are one in man. The reality of the spirit is its activity and the activity by which it knows the world or God is the activity by which man is ever creating these «objects.» Every act of knowing is a feeling or willing and every act of will is a knowing.[24]

However, as H.S. Harris points out, Gentile's use of the term «create» was an unfortunate choice. In order to express the united act of thought and will Gentile used the term «autoctisi» which Spaventa had «coined» from the Greek Fathers when they spoke of the «creation ex nihilo» by God. Harris feels that the term and the whole concept in Gentile should be translated as «self-founding» or «self-constitution.» and the term «constituting» or the term «positing» used to replace the term «create.» This point is well taken because Gentile himself often took great pains to explain what he meant by «create,» or better, what he did *not* mean by the term. In other words — Gentile did not mean that man gives entitative, real, extra-mental existence to God.[25]

Nevertheless, it would seem that a careful study of Gentile's works should make one realize that Gentile is not suggesting that there is an identification of the being of God and man. He is saying that pure consciousness, whether of God or the world, is an abstraction. True knowledge lies in a union of consciousness and self-consciousness and thus the reality known is self-generated. This is mediation, this is «self-consti-

[23] This basic theme runs all through German Idealism. See G. Santayana, *The German Mind*, N.Y.C., 1968. (Originally published in 1915 *as Egotism in German Philosophy*).

[24] Angelo Crespi, Contemporary Thought of Italy, p. 154.

[25] See H.S. Harris, *The Social Philosophy of Giovanni Gentile*, Urbana, Ill., 1960, p. 35 and p. 300.

tution,» and in it the opposition between knowing and making becomes purely ideal. The human spirit then knows what it has made willingly. Understanding anything other than ourselves would actually be understanding ourselves. Reality becomes the actual process of experience. [26]

These notions form the basis of the first two arguments for God's existence which shall now be presented. The third argument stems from statements which have been seen in the first and second chapters.

### 3.- PROOFS FOR GOD'S EXISTENCE

Gentile's specific arguments for God's existence can be reduced to the following three. The first is as follows:

Gentile argues that the existence of God is evident from the Bible, the Christian writings and the conviction of men down through the ages.

His writings are filled with the mention of the transcendent God as He is spoken of in Judaeo-Christian literature and as He has been universally accepted and believed in by people in all times and places. This shows that these beliefs are accepted by Gentile as a criterion for God's existence.

As each man thinks of the transcendent God, he posits Him as the non-self, a limit of the self. Consequently God becomes an ideal objective moment of the dialectical act of the transcendental self. In other words, God becomes clear and real for man through man's thinking.

However, since thinking and willing are one and the same act, thinking on God creates God because of the absolute liberty of the act. Thus God becomes absolutely immanent to the spiritual act of man. The serious man who seeks the truth about God will find this truth within himself, in his own creative pronouncement of His existence.

Therefore, for the sincere man, for man concretely or philosophically considered, God is not only real, He is, in a sense,

[26] *Sommario di pedagogia,* Vol. I, pp. 84-97.

each man's own creation. [27] The problem involved in this argument is to what extent man can be said to «create» God. For the discussion of this problem see Chapter VI.

The second argument which can be drawn from the writings of Gentile is very much like the first, although not exactly the same. It does not take the knowledge of the transcendent God as its starting point, but rather the finite self.

Gentile admits that each man is finite, existing in time and space. However, the act of self-consciousness recognizes the self as it is, notably, a finite self. Man can more deeply reflect on his own finitude and realize the need for the infinite. His reflective thinking tells him that his finite self supposes his infinite self. As man seeks to understand and overcome this finite condition, he responds to a profound moral need,

[27] Various specific texts can be cited in support of this argument which is a summation of Gentile's thought as expressed in the first two chapters and the first part of this chapter. The following texts, among others, support this argument:

*Teoria dello spirito*, p. 27: «Della realtà spirituale è da dire ciò che i grandi scrittori cristiani han detto di Dio: che la trova chi la cerca, e vuole perciò trovarla, e pone tutto il proprio essere in questa ricerca, come per appagare il più profondo bisogno della propria vita. Il Dio che potete trovare è quello che voi dovete far essere... .»

*Ibid.*, p. 259: Una realtà che è ora si veramente amore e volontà; perche è lo stesso sforzo interiore dell'anima, il suo vivo processo, non l'ideale suo e il suo modello esteriore; lo stesso uomo, che trasumana e si fa Dio. Non più il Dio che è già, ma il Dio che si genera in noi, ed è noi stessi, in quanto noi, con tutto l'esser nostro, ci eleviamo a lui. Qui lo spirito non è piu intelletto, ma volontà.»

*Discorsi di religione*, p. 140: «L'uomo che scopre in se Dio, e in certo modo lo crea, non è l'uomo naturale, ma l'uomo che è spirito... uomo ma anche Dio.»

*Introduzione alla filosofia*, p. 254: «Questo Dio che è padre ed è figlio, perchè è spirito, à trascendente o è immanente ? La risposta ora credo sia agevole... Di questa tracendenza, dico della trascendenza che sta a cuore ad ogni uomo sinceramente religioso, ce n'è quanta se ne vuole.»

*Ibid.*, p. 209: «La cui presenza desta l'interna vita dello spirito.

*Ibid.*, p. 205: «... l'autocoscienza in sè considerata non è meno infinita ed assoluta della Verità in sè considerata.»

not only of his own life, but a need of the wole of mankind. [28]

In this act of self-consciousness abstract man is overcome. In the logic of the concrete, our finite self is no longer deified by the belief that it truly knows God. For God becomes logically real within our pure act of thinking and not in the abstract, intellectual mode of thinking. It is each man's very nature as Truth which confers necessity and universality on our thought about God and not just the abstract, particular man. Through man's infinite and eternal act he overcomes his finite particularity. [29]

Thus we realize that the finite alone does not and cannot exist. Through the mediacy of thinking the finite becomes absolute. The existence of God, which is posited by the transcendental self cannot be doubted and thus atheism really becomes the denial of man, not God.

This argument may seem to lead a pantheistic conception of God but Gentile explicitly rejects such an accusation since he does not think that God and the transcendental ego are one. [30]

A third argument for God takes its starting point from empirical reality. Gentile states that there is a «unity which

[28] See citation on the preceeding page taken from the *Teoria generale dello spirito*, p. 27; also *Introduzione alla filosofia*, pp. 248-249: «Molti sono oggi che, a vedere, sarebbero tentati di abbracciarsi all'attualismo come all'unica fede che sia veramente idonea a sottrarre la mente agli argomenti e alle seduzioni del corrente materialismo... E sul punto di abbondonarsi a questa tentazione, che risponde a profondi bisogni morali del nostro tempo orientato universalmente verso una realtà conforme alle aspirazioni dello spirito...» See also Ugo Spirito's article on Gentile in the *Enciclopedia Italiana*, Vol. 16, p. 580: «Dio è immanente nell'atto spirituale e nè costituisce il momento ideale e oggettivo, il dover essere della deficiente realtà umana.»

[29] *Introduzione alla filosofia*, p. 201: «Questa personalità del Vero, che si attua logicamente nel nostro pensiero ... conferisce infatti al pensare quella necessità ed universalità per cui pensando secondo verità l'uomo vince la sua particolarità finita e spaziale nell'infinito e nell'eterno.»

[30] *Ibid.*, p. 205: «L'uomo come individuo tra individui, come essere naturale... e l'uomo dell'esperienza che suppone quell'Io, senza di cui parlare di esperienza non ha senso ... L'uomo creatura distinta dal suo Creatore è sempre oggetto del pensiero condizionato da questo Io trascendentale.»

underlies the multiplicity of experience» and metaphysics studies this unity and the relations of all things to each other. An examination of Nature makes us immediately aware of a harmony or orderliness, a system of laws to be found therein. Thus, the God who is always present in the depths of our hearts, is also present in the world before us. All things are ordered by the Being who is the foundation of this system and this Being is God. Therefore, Nature also tells us that God exists. [31]

The difference between the first two arguments and the third lies in the fact in the first two man ultimately discovers God within and through the creative act of the transcendental ego; in the third argument God is discovered in the world. With regard to this third argument it should be noted that Gentile does not give an explicitly developed reasoned process. His grasp of God in Nature is more immediate and intuitive than discursive, at least as far as it is expressed in his works. In his own mind such a process might well have existed. This reasoning process could be close to the hegelian process which admits mediacies linking different kinds of beings. Yet Gentile's excludes God's being pantheistically conceived or conceived as an Absolute underlying and uniting all kinds of beings.

[31] *Teoria dello spirito*, p. 151: «La metafisica è concezione dell'unità già giacente in fondo alla molteplicità dell'esperienza (quando, beninteso questa esperienza sia pensata).»

Two statements form the main basis for this third argument. They may be found above in Chapter I, p. 13 and in Chapter II, p. 42. In the latter statement there is also a brief mention made of an inner consciousness or personal feeling of God, a feeling which drives us on to discover Him. It is difficult to determine if God can be found only within our hearts or if this feeling is to aid our discovery of Him in the world. It is perhaps noteworthy, however, that the statement of the personal experience is immediately followed by the statement of the empirical or objective experience.

## SUMMARY

It might be noted that God, whether found in revelation, history or nature comes within the creative act of thinking. Therefore, all of Gentile's arguments are ultimately a fusion of the traditional «a priori» and «a posteriori» modes of demonstration.

Gentile's empirical approach to God amounts to an immediate grasp of the infinite in the finite. However, it would have been more satisfying if we had been given the reasoning process Gentile made provided there was such a process. The student of Gentile is left with the task of supplying the premises. However, since Gentile rejected the aristotelean syllogistic process perhaps an intuitive grasp of God, both within and without, is all that can be expected of him.

These criticisms and others will be developed in the final evaluation of Gentile's thought on God. Let us now examine his criticism of the attempts of his predecessors to demonstrate God's existence.

# CHAPTER IV

## GENTILE'S CRITIQUE OF THE CLASSIC VIEWS CONCERNING GOD

Having seen Gentile's own demonstration for the existence of God, we are now in a better position to appreciate his criticism of many of the classic arguments for God which preceeded the introduction of the logic of the concrete. Let us now examine his criticism of the metaphysical foundations of these arguments and the arguments themselves.

The philosophy of Giovanni Gentile was a very critical philosophy. Even a cursory reading of any of his major works would give evidence of a broad and careful consideration of the thought of philosophers of the past, both major and minor. Gentile's unique approach to God, as we saw summarized in his «new demonstration,» was made after he found all other demonstrations and concepts of God wanting. The universal problem, Gentile thinks, which every approach to God seemed to possess was an inability to shake off the influence of platonic-aristotelean philosophy. This is the case whether one is speaking of Anselm and Descartes on the one hand or of St. Thomas on the other. Even Kant and Hegel, according to Gentile, did not escape this influence on their basic thought. It seems strange because these men represent completely opposite poles of the epistemological-metaphysical spectrum.

It will be the aim of this chapter to show Gentile's criticism of some of the ways by which certain philosophers tried to come to the knowledge of God. We shall see why these seemingly varied approaches were rejected individually, although it is evident that the main reason lies in the different and unique theory of knowledge and being which Gentile had arrived at very early in his career. First of all, however, Gentile criticizes the basis of Plato's and Aristotle's intellectualism, which formed the basis for the traditional demonstrations for the existence of God.

## 1.- CRITIQUE OF GREEK INTELLECTUALISM

### a. *Critique of Transcendence in Plato.*

Gentile saw Plato and his prize pupil Aristotle as the main causes of most of the so-called great problems of philosophy, since every problem demands first of all the resolution of the problem of knowledge and truth. In this search for truth and the manner of discovering it, Gentile finds that Plato and Aristotle directed man's mind or consciousness away from itself to things outside of itself. The theory which took precedence was Aristotle's, which held that truth was mainly in the second act of the intellect, the judgment. The intellect pronounced the judgment, and if it corresponded to external reality, it was true; if not, it was false. The judgment was made up of concepts which were realities of the mind, thoughts. For Aristotle, then, truth lies in a relationship which transcends the mind's knowing power and depends on this mind's possessing the essence or quiddity of an object external to it and pronouncing on it. Gentile blames Plato for this external, objective element in the aristotelean realist school of thought because it was Plato who introduced the notion of a world or realm of realities which transcended the human thinking power. [1] Platonic mental realities were only copies of the Ideas which existed in a state of complete independence of man's mind or thinking process. If man was to possess the truth, his concepts and judments had to conform to the Ideas or their archetypes in the world. There was no freedom in this; no liberty or creative thinking. The thought of man had to be as sterile, immobile and static as the thing outside it. It had to remain an unproductive spectator.

[1] *Teoria generale dello spirito,* p. 43.

The dialectic for Plato was not what it was for Gentile. Plato's was a dialectic of «pensiero-pensato».[2] It was an inquiry into the internal relations among the separated Ideas inasmuch as they formed a sort of system. Plato's dialectic, according to Gentile, studied the universal and the particular and the relationship between the two. Philosophy became a study of mind as comprehensive, as taking in the concepts of and nature of all sciences and examining them in their individuality. Under the influence of the principle of identity of Parmenides, the Platonic is what it is and it cannot change in itself or be transformed in itself. Our knowledge of the Ideas and their relations can be deepened, but this supposes the fixity and immutability of the idea in itself.[2]

The human act of thinking has no real effect on the unity or multiplicity of the transcendental realm. For Gentile this kind of dialectic which Plato suggests is only an apparent dialectic because it presupposes a transcendent, external world. Reality, for Plato, is opposed to the thought which thinks it and thus an immediate knowledge results. This transcendentalism of the object and our knowledge of it is the true defect of the platonic dialectic.[3]

It is obvious from this explanation or criticism that it is based on Gentile's own concept of dialectic which is internal to the act of thinking and which unifies subject and object.

### b. *Critique of Aristotle and His Syllogistic.*

Although there can be some doubt among scholars as to whether or not Aristotle always accepted a realm of Ideas or Forms, Gentile at least finds fault with Aristotle's acceptance of platonic naturalism.[4] Whatever idealism or spiritual-

[2] *Ibid.*, p. 44.

[3] *Ibid.*, pp. 46-47.

[4] In his *History of Philosophy*, Vol. 1, part I, p. 195, COPLESTON questions what Aristotle meant by «separation» with regard to the Forms of Plato. H. WINDELBAND, however, holds that Aristotle did believe that the Forms had a separate existence (*History of Ancient Philosophy*, New York, 1956,

.sm is present in the thought of these two men is naturalistiq i.e., they consider reality to be a presupposition of the spirit.[5] Many Christian philosophers throughout the centuries made the mistake of thinking that Aristotle and especially Plato had defended the spirit in man because of their doctrine of intellect. However, they made the «spirit» a spectator of physical nature and it generated static, finite concepts which were tied down to the spatial and temporal. Knowing was opposed to willing and loving; therefore, spontaneous creativity, liberty, the infinite and eternal act of self-consciousness were never fully and validly appreciated. Because of this opposition between subject and object as well as between knowing and willing, Greek philosophy excluded us from a true grasp of reality. Greek intellectualistic conceptions, when making external reality a condition of our knowing, destroyed our divine humanity, which transcends the empirical self. Greek philosophy tended to lead us away from the «imago Dei,» the «Deus in nobis» which Augustine suspected and Kant brought out.[6]

Aristotle, according to Gentile, did deny the platonic transcendence of Forms, but he made the Ideal Forms immanent to matter, so as to bring from and matter together. However, even Aristotle believed our mind thinks of nature as antecedent to thought, as «reality already realized.» The mind of man had the function of discovering essences and so forming fixed definitions. Science is an act of the intellect which tries to discover the movement in the world caused by the final cause or prime mover of the world. But this movement, this aristotelean «becoming,» is not a becoming of thought. As a presupposition it supplies us with one thought after another, a multitude, but each a «pensiero pensato.» Their meaning

pp. 247-248 and p. 257, tr. by H. Cushman). Gentile says that Aristotle denied the transcendence of the Forms (*Teoria generale dello spirito*, p. 48).

[5] *Ibid.*, p. 47. Cf. *supra*, Ch. I, pp. 12-13. The term «logo» for Gentile means «reality in its intelligibility» and he tells us that his «logo» is the pure act of knowing. See the *Sistema di logica*, Vol. 1, p. 20.

[6] *Sistema di logica*, Vol. 1, pp. 20-26; *Discorsi di religione*, pp. 27-48.

and their internal relations correspond to the dialectic of the transcendent Ideas of Plato, and their internal dialectic is just as meaningless. Therefore, the intellect and its acts are not truly indicative of the life of the spirit in man.[7]

Aristotle, nevertheless, went beyond the platonic identity of subject and predicate in the judgment. This was an abstract immediacy. Aristotle developed the syllogism in which the subject is not immediately identical with the predicate but rather with a third term (the middle term) which is also shown to be identical with the predicate. The syllogism was implicit in the dialectic of Plato but the important difference lies in the fact that Aristotle saw a need for mediacy, i.e., a «mediation between the being which thinks and that which it is able to think.»[8] However, the aristotelean syllogism runs into various difficulties. For one, the middle term becomes simply another «pensiero pensato,» a fixed concept, a new nature, an «object of thought,» the result being that we do not have a cognitive process but only a system which deals with objects of knowledge. We do not have authentic mediation but only a mediate term or concept. The syllogism closes in upon itself and we have only a triadic complexity of static concepts based upon presuppositions and governed by certain laws. We have a formal scheme (formal logic) hopefully stemming from the intellect's acquisition of knowledge of nature (material logic). The result is truly immediacy. This is abstract logical procedure. In addition to these two problems the syllogism suffers from the problem of the universal truth at which it must arrive in at least one of its premises, and his involves the problem of induction. Gentile asks: «If I know that Socrates is an animal because 'every man is an animal,' am I not caught up in circular reasoning? Did I not have to know my conclusion in order to know my premise?»[9] There is the great danger of a «petitio principii» here and Gentile declares that this is a very

[7] *Teoria generale dello spirito,* pp. 48-49.
[8] *Sistema di logica,* Vol. 1, p. 161.
[9] *Ibid.,* pp. 249-250. For a detailed examination of GENTILE's view see the *Sistema di logica,* Vol. 1, Chapter 6, and Vol. 2, pp. 3-27.

«exact criticism.» These criticisms, therefore, place a grave doubt on the ability of the aristotelean syllogistic process to arrive deductively at new truth. For Gentile we may say that it is philosophically without value.

## 2.- CRITIQUE OF THE FIRST PRINCIPLES OF REALITY

### a. *Critique of the Principles of Identity and non-Contradiction.*

Gentile's critique of these principles is not completely unfavorable. Although a complete study of his critique would go beyond the scope and purpose of this work, it should be considered because of the fact that these principles take on a special value in themselves as standing alone for the proofs of God's existence in Gentile's approach to God: that is, Gentile sees these principles as having their origin in the Greek philosophical tradition — especially from the thought of Parmenides and Aristotle. He realizes that they are considered to be the first principles of knowledge or of the «speculative order» as the scholastics would say. Gentile speaks of these principles in some of his works but since they are principles of the logic of the abstract, «the indispensable condition of thought» for Plato and Aristotle, [10] he holds that they are not valid in themselves to demonstrate the existence of God.

However, Genile believes that they can be used in both an abstract manner and in a concrete manner. By «abstract manner» Gentile understands their ordinary usage, namely, their static opposition or identity between subject and object or between objects alone. By «concrete manner» is meant the way in which Gentile uses them, namely, as resulting in the principle of the excluded third because of our thinking's synthetic unification of the whole of reality.

In his demonstration for God's existence he gives us one of our best insights into his position on these principles. He

[10] *Teoria generale dello spirito,* p. 44.

shows us that Greek philosophy wasn't all bad because Socrates had begun to conceive of «intelligibility» or the «ideality of reality.» [11] Unfortunately, the Greeks seemed enchanted with immobility — immobility of man's idea of the Ideas. This would explain the importance given to the principle of identity: A=A. Herein, truth is evident and necessary. The principle of non-contradiction flows from this when we say: A is not non-A. Thus we have a profound division between the concept of «thought thought» for which the principle of non-contradiction has a sense and that of thought thinking, i.e., the act of the transcendental Self for which the principle of non-contradiction has no application. The world as thought (pensato) can only be thought of as immutable. However, this is a new world, the day of a new logic. The principles of identity and non-contradiction are only abstract terms of man's transcendental thinking activity. [12] For Gentile, they are no longer of themselves the «columns of Hercules» which they once were in the Greek-Scholastic tradition. These principles should not be treated as anterior to our thinking and therefore independent of it. The principle of identity receives logical signification when it is understood as non-contradiction. The latter principle is its logical complement. In thinking that «A is not the same as non-A,» I give the principles their truth. I pronounce also that between being and non-being there is nothing, there is no third. In this mediation truth and significance are being given by the transcendental self's pure act of thinking. In the pronouncing of the «principle of the excluded third,» we have the position of the logic of the concrete. For Gentile, then, the principles of identity and non-contradiction are the abstract forms, or ideal moments of the «full and effective form which is the concrete form. The principle of the excluded third is the living synthesis or organic unity of the two preceding principles, themselves understood as true in that synthesis.» [13] Without this resolution or assertion by the

[11] *Introduzione alla filosofia*, p. 195.

[12] *Teoria generale dello spirito*, p. 45; *Introduzione alla filosofia*, pp. 196-197.

[13] *Introduzione alla filosofia*, p. 197.

act of thinking the abstractness of these principles cannot be overcome. Their truth lies in the act by which we become aware of the difference between being and non-being and the exclusion of a third. In this positing of the «no-third» the infinite and absolute Person is revealed. [14]

b. *Critique of the Principle of Causality.*

Gentile feels that the metaphysical concept of causality, as conceived by the rationalist philosopher, Spinoza, and the empiricist philosopher, Hume, and by those who attemted to unite their basic concepts, is useless in philosophy. Gentile sees metaphysical causalty as possessing an absolute relationhip between condition (condizione) and conditionate (condizionato), that is, one cannot think of either one (cause or effect) without thinking of the other. The absolute character of this relation and the necessity of following the condionate back to the condition makes up the constitutive elements of the metaphysical concept of cause «which can be defined as that reality the realization of which renders necessary the realization of another reality.» [15] Gentile, however, points out that here we do not have the simple succession of empirical causality; rather we have what Gentile refers to as a necessary and sufficient condition in which the cause is necessary for the effect and the effect is necessary for the cause. The

[14] *Ibid.*, pp. 198-199.

[15] *Teoria generale dello spirito*, pp. 150-151 and 154-155. The sense of these pages is that the principle of efficient causality as traditionally used is not valid. It possesses both a rational and empirical element. I don't believe that the scholastics held it to be a purely a priori principle nor that it was based on the perception of mere succession. Gentile rejected each aspect in itself and the combination of the two. Gentile felt that Spinoza made the principle a mere logical deduction which was founded on the principle of identity, and that Hume made the relationship between cause and effect a mere empirical consequence. Gentile saw the former as an abstractly rationalistic and intellectualistic position while the latter leads to obscurity and scepticism and ends up in absolute multiplicity.

reciprocal necessity of conceiving one term together with the other is a necessary consequence of the realization of cause. When this happens, however, the concepts or terms are no longer two but one. Gentile points out that if the terms are God and the world, we must have pantheism. We would have metaphysical identity. In «efficient causality» the reality of the effect issues «from the womb» of the reality of the cause, but «it is obvious,» Gentile declares, «that this is nothing but the intellectualistic and abstractly rationalisic position of a metaphysics like that of Spinoza,» who tried to construct the real world on the basis of substance (causa sui) whose essence implies existence. [16] This is not a case wherein one can think of the effect without thinking of the cause at the same time, e.g., God can be without the world, but the world cannot be without God. [17]

Metaphysics, for Gentile, is «the conception of unity lying at the base of the multiplicity of experience» (when experience is thought). Metaphysics has in it the possibility of all the different and varied forms to be found in nature and is the principle of them. This is why the Being of Parmenides or the Ideas of Plato are metaphysical — they are unities to which all empirical things can be reduced.

Empirical causality, on the other hand, involves simple succession and deals only with contingent facts in physical nature. Metaphysical and empirical causality are extreme opposites. They are like a «two-headed Janus» with one side looking toward metaphysical unity and necessity in order to resolve the problems of empiricism and the other side looking toward diversity and fact in order to complement metaphysical rationality. Again, unity and multiplicity are extreme opposites. The metaphysical concept of causality is absurd because «the concept of condition in fact carries with it the concept of the

[16] *Ibid.*, p. 154.

[17] It should be noted here that for Gentile man considered as finite is caused by God but that man in a certain way «creates God» (see above Chapter I, p. 35). In his *Teoria generale dello spirito* he tells us that the God that any man finds is the God whom in seeking he makes to be (p. 49).

duality of condition and conditionate, i.e., the possibility of conceiving each term without the other.» This is a possibility by the metaphysical apriority of causal relation, which, as we have seen, carried with it the identity and unity of the two terms. Therefore, since duality is not identity, «to speak of causality in the metaphysical sense is to say... something which makes no sense.» Gentile sees us as ending up with a «reciprocal relative necessity,» or absolute necessity excluding every contingency. [18] His critique concludes:

> Between the unity, therefore, of metaphysics and the multiplicity of empiricism every attempt to establish a relationship of condition (cause) and conditionate (effect) as a relationship which mediates between unity and multiplicity is doomed to failure. [19]

The rationalistic and intellectualistic metaphysics of beings with essences, natures and powers belongs to empirical and abstract philosophical positions. Only therein does such metaphysics have some value. On the other hand it should be noted that Gentile's own system estiblishes a kind of unity on the basis of the synthesizing activity of actual thinking.

### 3.- CRITIQUE OF THE ARGUMENT OF ST. ANSELM

Gentile posits at least five objecions to St. Anselm's argument as outlined in the *Proslogium I.* St. Anselm, in his famed «ontological argument,» fell into the typical errors of subject and object, inside and outside, that which is internal to think-

[18] *Ibid.,* p. 160. For example we would say that since we have a body there must be a God to create the soul for that body, or that since every monad supposes a God creator of all monads there must be other monads, etc. (Gentile's examples).

[19] *Ibid.,* p. 160: «Tra l'unità, dunque, della metafisica e la molteplicità dell'empirismo ogni sforzo di fissare un rapporto di condizione e condizionato, come rapporto che medii tra l'unità e la molteplicità, è destinato di fallire.»

ing and that which is external to the understanding.[20] This leads him into the problem of truth — does anything external to my act of understanding correspond to that which is in my understanding. Anselm is seeking an «adequation» between his judgment and external reality.[21]

Gentile's third objection is that Anselm used the aristotelean syllogism and this led him into a «peitio principii.» While Gentile is not precise here as to premises, he seems to mean that the conclusion had to be known and used in order to posit the second or minor premise, namely, God exists because He is that greater than which nothing can be thought of, and therefore cannot exist in the understanding alone.[23]

Gentile's fourth objection is that God is for Anselm a «pensiero pensato» Who already exists in the understanding because of Anselm's faith.[24] Anselm is incapable of avoiding the union of theology and philosophy, a union in which philosophy is subordinated to theology, a union in which philosophy is subordinated to theology and its dogmas.[24] Anselm remains trapped in the Greek tradition of the fixcd Being of Parmenides and Ideas of Plato. Since this is the case, Gentile's fifth difficulty is the simple inability of Anselm to answer «the fool» or Gaunilon's defense of «the fool.» Anselm was like all the other scholastics who tried to answer «the fool» of the psalm with the platonic or aristotelean concept of spirit, namely, with the immaterial intellect and its various acts.[25] According to Gentile the concept of spirit must understand spirit as creative and productive of its object, not just an understanding spectator. Anselm lacked insight into the liberty of believing. Gentile believes that he failed to see that

[20] G. Gentile, *I problemi della scholastica,* Bari, 1913, p. 68.

[21] *Ibid.,* p. 65.

[22] *Ibid.,* p. 68.

[23] *Ibid.,* p. 59. Gentile believes that the contention that understanding demanded belief was a mentality within which all neo-platonists philosophized.

[24] *Il modernismo,* p. 112: «Quindi il rapporto, accennato già in S. Anselmo, è formulato esplicitamente in tutti le somme degli scolastici posteriori, di subordinazione della filosofia alla teologia.»

[25] *I problemi della scolastica,* pp. 68-69.

believing and knowing are the same thing and, therefore, takes the intellect on an act of faith and makes knowing a divine act. [26]

### 4.- CRITIQUE OF THE ARGUMENT OF ST. BONAVENTURE

Gentile's critique of St. Bonaventure is somewhat more detailed and precise than that of St.Anselm, although he finds much the same difficulties. Throughout these criticisms of the so-called neo-platonists or neo-aristoteleans, he is constantly making a comparison between their approach to God and his own. Generally he feels that the medieval thinkers were not really philosophers. We shall consider this at the end of the chapter.

Gentile sees St. Bonaventure, like all scholastics, primarily as a theologian and a follower of the neo-platonic tradition of philosophy. Bonaventure, like St. Thomas, feels forced to look beyond himself to find God. The human intellect must be illumined by God in order to understand any truth, including the truth of God's existence. [27] Both of the afore-mentioned men followed the lead of St. Anselm and the platonic motto: Credo ut intelligam. [28] St. Bonaventure, by considering the degrees of perfections, [29] also philosophized in a genuine aristotelean spirit because he distinguished between «something in matter» and «another thing.» Gentile holds that Aristotle himself was led from form to form and finally to his God who was a form supreme and transcendent. Neither Bonaventure, St. Thomas nor their contemporaries escaped this Greek influence. [30]

Like Anselm, Bonaventure also used a reasoning process. The proof, Gentile points out, is platonic because the concepts or

[26] *Ibid.*, p. 65.

[27] *Ibid.*, p. 58; see also *Il modernismo*, p. 112.

[28] *Ibid.*, p. 59.

[29] Gentile is referring to the argument of the *Itinerarium Mentis ad Deum*, III, 3.

[30] *Ibid.*, p. 47 and p. 58: «... ma per Kant la verità nostra à nostra; e per Tommaso, in fondo, non è propriamente nostra. Perché è fundamento di

ideas which we find existing in our mind make up the matter of the proof. We have to explain them as they are, i.e., as representational of a maximum. This would seem to reduce the proof to the use of the principle of natural causality wherein both cause and effort are natural and contingent. Bonaventure was looking for his cause outside of the intellect and superior to it. What he never came to, we are told by Gentile, is that the necessity in a logical process lies in the process, not in the matter. He also misses the absolute autonomy of the affirmations of the human spirit. For Bonaventure truth must come to us from the outside. This creates an absurd problem.[31] The use of the reasoning process limits Bonaventure to the Greek and medieval traditions and prevents him from attaining to the modern approach which is the approach of true immanence.

Although Gentile finds the grades or steps of the journey of the mind to God (the «Itinerarium») to be «laborious,» he does hold that St. Francis himself revived the spirit of the divine in man. The love of the subject for God and the supreme peace of the spirit of which the fransciscan mystical writers spoke was unknown to the Greeks.[32] In spite of this Bonaventure, like all christian theologians, had difficulty translating this love and will into a theory whereby our God is the God which each man makes rather than man being only that which God makes.[33]

tutti i giudizi dell'intelletto, che tolgono la loro materia dal senso e però sono una produzione di esso intelletto...». And on p. 59: «Anche Tommaso, come Bonaventura, e costretto qui a trascendere *semetipsum.* L'intelletto per la luce di queste fondamentali verità, onde poi rilucono tutte le altre, dev'essere illuminato da Dio.» Here Gentile sees St. Thomas as taking his thought from both the aristotelean and platonic traditions, hence weakening his immanentistic insights.

31 *Ibid.,* p. 46.

32 *Ibid.,* pp. 46-47; see also pp. 33-35. BONAVENTURE, in the *Itinerarium Mentis ad Deum,* chapter 3, mentions that the way to christian peace lies in the most ardent love of Christ crucified. The franciscan soul should be absorbed in Christ.

33 *Ibid.,* p. 35.

The true franciscan soul of Bonaventure was «crushed» due to the scholastic influences of his time. His vision was «obscured.» The God for whom he was searching could only be a passive intuition of something external to the subject. Since his purpose was to discover the action of God on the human intellect, Bonaventure was never able to have a union with God that was truly autonomous and active. [34] In addition, his mystical tendencies, through which man is absorbed in God at the end of his «itinerarium,» cause man to lose his selfhood in this all-encompassing presence of the transcendent God... This was indicated by St. Paul when he said: «Vivo autem, jam non ego; vivit vero in me Christus.»

Thus we see that two of the most famous early medieval and medieval neo-platonic approaches to God, the Anselmian and Bonaventurean, were not, for Gentile, considered satisfactory to Gentile. Let us now see his critique of the medieval approach of St. Thomas Aquinas, which shares the aristotelean and platonic traditions.

## 5.- CRITIQUE OF ST. THOMAS AQUINAS

### a. *Critique of the «Five Ways.»*

As we have seen, Gentile believed that platonic philosophers like Bonaventure and Anselm who held that God is an innate idea and remained enclosed within their faith in the objectivity of the idea of God, made their philosophical thesis coincide with the immediacy of their credo. Their point of departure was their theory of innate ideas. No demonstration was needed because their conclusion was their principle; therefore, no thought process was possible. [35]

St. Thomas Aquinas, thanks to the influence of Albertus Magnus and Aristotle, did not believe the ontological argument of Anselm to be valid. Gentile points out that St. Thom-

[34] *Ibid.*, p. 49.

[35] *I problemi della scolastica*, pp. 74-75; see also p. 74, where Gentile accuses Bonaventure and platonically inclined philosophers: «... i filosofi

as, whom he held to be the greatest speculative intellect of the thirteenth century, did not believe that man could move to God from a concept of God but must begin with things and the sensation of things. St. Thomas, according to Gentile, had a definite aversion to dualism and to transcendence. Together with St. Albert he pointed out the true realism — moderate realism.[36] In his attempt to demonstrate God's existence from a consideration of the world, St. Thomas at least avoided extreme platonic transcendence even if he did begin with aristotelean sensation («an obscure act of the psyche,» according to Gentile). Gentile believes that St. Thomas rejected the theory that truth is outside the intellect: this is to St. Thomas' great credit, since this theory was an attempt to make a return to the spirit. Thought possessed an internal coherence creating itself by apprehending and judging. The human spirit thereby possesses and procures the peace of God, and this is the profound intuition of thomism, genuinely mystical and Christian.[37]

Nevertheless, St. Thomas, like Bonaventure, was constrained to transcend his own thinking and go to the world of nature for his primary phenomena. St. Thomas began with the concretized aristotelean forms and considered these material entities as movers and causes, contingent, participated and finalized in his famous «five ways.»[38] From the physical and finite he attempted to demonstrate the metaphysical and infinite reality of God.

In his critique on scholastic philosophy, Gentile first makes

*platonizzanti* come Bonaventura ammettendo di Dio un idea innata...;» and on p. 59 of the same work Gentile refers to Anselm as: «... il *platonizzante* Anselmo d'Aosta...».

[36] G. Gentile, *Storia della filosofia italiana,* Firenze, 1961, p. 69: «Tommaso d'Aquino con la sua decisa avversione al dualismo e alla trascendenza non partecipa nè alla veduta dell'uno nè a quella dell'altro di codesti opposti indirizzi.» I believe that Gentile is speaking of platonic transcendence here. However, he could be clearer in his assertion about «dualism,» since St. Thomas did distinguish God from the world and the soul from the body even though he considered man to be a unity.

[37] *I problemi della scolastica,* p. 57.

[38] St. Thomas Aquinas, *Summa Theol.,* I, 2, 3.

a brief summation of St. Thomas' criticism of the ontological argument [39] and then begins a consideration of the «five ways.» Gentile felt that the development of these «ways» to God was the pride of St. Thomas' lifelong effort to know God. However, he thought that the aristotelean-platonic influences on St. Thomas were too strong and that his theory of truth and cognition was fraught with the logic of the absract and the doctrine of immediacy in knowledge.

The «first way,» Gentile points out, is based on the aristotelean theory of motion and follows the outline of Aristotle's advance toward the Prime Mover. It creates a problem which St. Thomas was to have with him throughout all five ways. First of all, the first way leads us to a Prime Mover who is pure movement and lives what life he possesses apart from the world. His absolute perfection seems to be in his absolute transcendence. Secondly, his argument from motion in the physical world creates an absolutely mechanistic system which is «certainly absurd.» The Prime Mover somehow moves everything in nature but as «pure movement stripped of all material forms,» it is broken off from the matter of nature; yet this God must live in nature and its hierarchy of forms. However, since the pure movement or immobility of God is not identical with the movement of matter, the life of nature excludes the divine life. If one were to ask how Aristotle and St. Thomas passed from nature to God, Gentile would answer that they never did. In spite of the thomistic distinction between nature and God, the fact remains that movement is of the essence of God, and when one speaks of nature, one speaks of God. One's contact with nature gives one a contact with God which is immediate. God, then, is not really demonstrated, and therefore, the «first way» is nothing more and nothing less than the ontological argument of Anselm; this in its turn is not a demonstration because God is immediately encountered in the intellect. [40]

[39] *I problemi della scolastica,* p. 76. Gentile feels that St. Thomas' criticism was valid. The «first way» is briefly considered in GENTILE's *Storia della filosofia italiana,* p. 75.

[40] *Ibid.,* p. 78: «Egli e che non vedono nella natura se no Dio (la natura

The «second way» uses the term «cause,» but it might just as well have used the term «mover.» St. Thomas reduces every effect in he universe to movement. Therefore, Gentile concludes, we find that all we have is another formulation of the «first way,» and the second attempt is no morc valid than the first. [41]

Gentile joins his criticism of the «third way» to that of the «fifth.» The «third way,» which says that we cannot go to infinity in contingent causes of the contingent, is mechanistic. Gentile feels that there is really no difference between the mechanism of the first three arguments and the principle of finality of the fifth. Finality for him is nothing but an upside-down mechanism. Mechanism is the world viewed externally, from without. Finality is the world viewed from within, in its interior life or being. Each view culminates with a mover which is external to the world. [42] God as end must be outside of every material form including the human soul; He must be outside of every material structures so that they may tend toward Him. Since St. Thomas has to uphold the doctrine of St. Paul, namely, that the invisible things of God can be known from the visible things of the world, [43] he created a deep abyss between God and the world. Gentile asserted that the essence of the «fifth way» as well as the similes of the archer and his arrow dig this abyss even deeper than the other arguments. [44]

Finally, the critique of the «fourth way» is very brief. The ascent from the imperfect possession of perfections in nature [45]

per loro e appunto quello stesso movimento, che e l'essenza divina); e quando han posto la natura, han posto, eo ipso Dio. Dio torna da capo ad essere un mero immediato, e non un dimostrato; ne piu, ne meno che l'argomento ontologico; un per se notum, malgrado la distinzione tomista.»

[41] *Ibid.*, p. 79.

[42] This is seen in the *Physics*, Bk. VII, and the *Metaphysics*, Bk. XII, of Aristotle, which Gentile calls «Aristotelean theology.»

[43] St. Paul, *Romans*, I, 20.

[44] *I problemi della scolastica*, p. 83.

[45] *Ibid.*, p. 81.

to the Perfect is a theological proof according to Gentile, although he doesn't tell us what he means by «theological.» He tells us that it falls into a mechanism and, like the others, brings us to a God who, in order to be what He is, could not be the cause of the world as we know it. If this God possessed all perfections in an absolute manner, then the world would have to be deprived of every perfection; if this were the case, the stairway to God which is presented by the fourth way would be broken. Therefore, a perfect God implies no perfections in a world distinct from God, and if his world lacked these grades of perfection, we could not use them to go to God. St. Thomas is on the horns of a dilemma from which he cannot extricate himself without falling into a pantheism, and this too is a choice he cannot make. [46]

In summation it might be pointed out that Gentile does not address himself to the thomistic doctrine of «participation of Being» nor is he precise in telling us what he means by «mechanism.» In a gesture of kindness he tells us that St. Thomas was simply a victim of his era. Had he been allowed to follow up his intuition of immanence, he would be held in even greater esteem than he is by modern philosophers. This leads us into the more serious problem that Gentile found in St.Thomas — the fact that St. Thomas was primarily a Catholic theologian.

### b. *Critique of the Negative Influence of Theology.*

Gentile was not at all happy with the negative control of theology over philosophy which was adhered to by Christian philosophers «up to the end of the middle ages.» For St. Thomas, as for many others, the reason of man and its conclusions must not contradict the dogmas of the Church which have come from the authority of divine revelation or the teaching Magisterium of the Church. God confers on man's reason a

[46] Gentile believed that this «way» was the same as the argument of St. Anselm in the *Monologium*.

double perfection — its natural light and the theological virtue of faith by which our reason is made worthy to attain to a superior grade of truth which transcends the powers of our natural reason This faith supposes our natural reason and the truths of God's existence and attributes which we are supposedly able to demonstrate through reason alone are not «articuli fidei, sed praeambula ad articulos.»[47] St. Thomas believed that even though human reason could not attain to supreme truth which is the object of theology, it has the negative power to confront the objections one might pose against theology. In human disputations philosophy can come to the aid of theology, it can be considered a necessary complement of theology. In other words, the medieval thinkers saw philosophy as the penetration or deepening of our knowledge of the nature of Christian mysteries. They sought to show why a mystery existed. They did not hope for a solution.

Gentile concludes that in spite of all the problems St. Thomas faced, he was no less a philosopher than he was a theologian. Gentile was saddened that St.Thomas was caught up in the web of transcendence that was so characteristic of scholastic philosophy, as well as the limitation placed upon human reason by this constant concern lest he contradict theological dogmas of his faith. Religion is only a moment of the life of the spirit and St. Thomas allowed his theological position to restrict his reasoning power to «a role which was purely negative, concerned with the refutation of error and denying it the positive activity of the creation of truth.» This is Gentile's main criticism of St. Thomas, although he admits that it is to the great credit of St. Thomas to have «neatly separated the dominion of reason and faith.»[48]

[47] *Ibid.*, p. 44. Gentile is citing the *Summa Theol.*, I, 2, 2 ad 1.

[48] *Storia della filosofia italiana*, p. 47: «Il valore adunque di Tomasso non è minore in filosofia che in teologia o, almeno egli non è meno filosofo che teologo. Ma bisogna pur convenire che una grande e recisa limitazione egli poneva alla libertà della ragione, restringendo l'assoluta potenza di questa alla parte puramente negativa di confutazione dell'errore, e negandole l'attività positiva di creazione della verità.» (Tr. mine.)

## 6.- SPECIFIC CRITIQUE OF SHOLASTIC PHILOSOPHY

By now it should be evident that, for Gentile, those thinkers who ordinarily fall under the heading of scholastics or neo-scholastics are not truly philosophers, i.e., they are not philosophers who really could fit into the modern era.
Whether they are augustinians, thomists, scotists, etc., they have made God an object of abstract speculation. The scholastic philosopher seeks to know and love God, whereas «the modern recreates Him in his very self.» The scholastic is «ignorant of the treasure which is within his own soul and looks for God... outside of himself, «whereas «the modern philosopher re-enters within himself and labors there... and knows the world with his own feelings.» [49]

The scholastics, including even St. Thomas, were never able to break away from the platonic-aristotelean epistemology in which consciousness is not considered as an activity of the subject but the end of the activity — objective consciousness, conformity, adequation. [50] God is transcendent object comparable to the platonic Form of the Good which illumines our minds. Scholastic doctrine demands the «principle of transcendence» and the «method of immanence.» However, scholastic «immanence» demands the finding of God in finite subjects, in the empirical or natural realm and the only result of such a theory is agnosticism. Scholastic philosophy contains no true doctrine of immanence nor a true idealism. Its idealism is «static, intellectualistic, and governed by the ideal of an absolutely eternal, objective truth of which man is but a spectator.» [51]

Christian theology intellectualizes or naturalizes the original spirit of the Christian religion. The doctrine of revelation cordesponds to the platonic theory reminiscence; human knowing, even the knowing of God, is something passive or intuitive, immediate. God becomes everything, man nothing.

[49] *Il modernismo*, p. 61.
[50] *I problemi della scolastica*, p. 89.
[51] *Il modernismo*, p. 36.

As we shall soon see, even the great modern philosophers did not escape these accusations. In the case of the scholastics like St. Thomas and St. Bonaventure, it might be noted that Gentile's exposition of their arguments for God's existence was not detailed and in St. Thomas' case did not show the use of the principle of contradiction in terms of potency and act. However, since such a method, together with the aristotelean theory of cognition belongs to the logic of the abstract, we have seen that this approach is not philosophically valid for actual idealism. Gentile ridicules the neo-scholastics for thinking that they have risen from their slumber and joined the twentieth century, when in reality «their philosophy remains that of the thirteenth century.»[52] The human intellect and its operations do not for Gentile, reveal the life of the human spirit, and this would seem to be scholasticism's greatest fault.

## 7.- CRITIQUE OF THE CARTESIAN «ONTOLOGICAL ARGUMENT»

Whether one considers Descartes to be the first of the great modern philosophers or the last of the great scholastics, he does not completely escape Gentile's criticism. At first Gentile remarks favorably that the ontological proof of God was brought into the modern era by Descartes, who, by his «cogito ergo sum,» for the first time filled in the terrible dualism of being and thought. The concreteness of the individual coincides with thought in its universality.[53]

However, the insistence, even of Descartes, on the discussion of the ontological argument shows that men have not been satisfied with it. Descartes faltered in his third Meditation and fell into the trap of the innatism of ideas, Greek

[52] *Ibid.*, p. 130.

[53] *Teoria generale dello spirito*, p. 72. Gentile praises Descartes' first turning from a «cogitatum» to the «cogitare» itself which would be an act of the self. Gentile felt that Descartes found the positive being of the individual in the «cogitare.» See the same source, p. 97.

transcendence and intellectualism.[54] God becomes an idea which tells Descartes of God's extra-mental reality, and this shows that Descartes is still under the medieval dualism of intellect and reality. If one tries to demonstrate God's existence by using either the ontological argument or some other argument, he will no doubt run into the difficulty of the anselmian argument. Therefore, one might well ask Descartes as well as all his predecessors: «How can an intellectual argument attain to anything other than an intellectual reality?» Nevertheless, it can still be said that Gentile was pleased with the idealistic beginning present in the «cogito.»

In summarizing Gentile's criticism of the proofs for God's existence offered by his predecessors, we may say that Gentile criticized them from the point of view of his basic principles. The method of immanence does not tolerate points of departure which are extrinsic to the act of thinking, not even concepts, and certainly not transcendent reality. He also rejected the traditional conception of the principle of efficient causality. He reaffirmed his own conviction that God must somehow be the product of human causality, the product of human thinking, and in that sense immanent to the act of thinking, but not to thought.

The philosophers who have tried to prove God's existence have sometimes been placed in either the neo-platonic or neo-aristotelean tradition or lineage of philosophy. For the neo-platonist God is an idea of the mind and this or some idea like that of participated perfection and its maximum would have God, not man, as its cause. For these thinkers God is a presupposition of their thought, He is something comparable to the Form of the Good which is a transcendent presupposition of thought Neo-aristoteleans fall essentially into the same error. God is a transcendent presupposition who is discovered immediately through sensation and intellectual abstraction together with the application of the first principles of knowledge. Even Vico and Kant made nature a creation of God and did not completely appreciate the elements of the logic of the

[54] *Ibid.*, p. 99.

concrete and the reflective-creative activity of the transcendental self. Therefore, all such attempts to arrive at the God of modern philosophy failed.

Let us now consider the significance of Gentile's position. For this purpose we shall treat first Gentile's originality in his basic thought and in his teaching on God and then the value and acceptability of his position.

# CHAPTER V

# THE ORIGINALITY OF GENTILE'S POSITION

Now that we have considered Gentile's position on the arguments for God's existence, the question arises as to his intellectual heritage and the degree of originality in his thought. Consequently, we shall treat of the influences on his arguments, particularly those of Vico and Spinoza, Kant and Hegel, and finally Fichte and Spaventa. From these influences we shall try to determine to what extent Gentile is original. Keep in mind the fact that Gentile's doctrine was also subject to influences on him in his own time.

## 1.- INFLUENCES ON GENTILE'S THOUGHT

### a. *Vico and Spinoza.*

As we mentioned in the Introduction and first chapter, Gentile, as a young man, came under the influence of Donato Jaja, a professor of philosophy at the University of Pisa. Jaja's main contribution to Gentile's intellectual formation was the introduction of Gentile to the thought of the neo-hegelean philosopher, Bertrando Spaventa. Gentile rarely mentions Jaja in his writings, but rather gives greater recognition to Jaja's teacher, Spaventa, and to the master of both — Hegel himself. In following the intellectual path of Jaja and Spaventa, Gentile renounced the positivistic philosophy rampant in Italy in the nineteenth century, as well as a career in literary studies. He became excited at the prospect of continuing the idealist tradition of philosophy along the lines of some of the insights of Spaventa.

Together with his enthusiasm for the idealist tradition or

philosophical viewpoint, Gentile was a fervent nationalist. He loved Italy and things Italian. He loved its past and wrote devotedly of the great thinkers who made up its intellectual heritage. His «tesi di laurea» was written on the Italian philosophers Rosmini and Gioberti, although he rarely refers to these men and did not find his major insights in their thought. The Italian whom he frequently refers to is Gianbattista Vico-(1668-1724).[1]

The texts of Vico to which Gentile makes his most frequent references are the 1710 work, *De antiquissima Italorum sapientia,* and the *Scienza nuova* (1725). Gentile tells us that the first work contains a profound truth in the famous motto, «verum et factum convertuntur,» which for Gentile conveys the meaning that the concept of truth coincides with the concept of fact; that the true is that which becomes. In his *Scienza nuova* Vico also states that history, considered in its entire process, replaces metaphysics as the object of philosophy. Gentile was pleased to see that Vico recognized his (Gentile's) own theory that history or the historical process is the development of the human spirit and that the human mind itself is the primary cause of all historical events. Men have disposed the causes for the production of events.[2]

Gentile also pointed out that Vico rejected immediacy as valid experience. Immediate knowledge was a contradiction in terms.[3] Although Gentile felt that there were skeptical strains in the *De antiquissima Italorum sapientia,* he decided that what Vico really meant and what he should have said in order to make himself perfectly correct was: «verum et *fieri* convertuntur» — that the fact which is convertible with the

[1] For example, in *Teoria generale dello spirito,* p. 19, Gentile refers to him as: «Il nostro Gianbattista Vico» («Our Italy's Gianbattista Vico»).

[2] *Teoria generale dello spirito,* pp. 19-20. See also the article on Gentile by Ugo Spirito in the *Enciclopedia Italiana,* Vol. XVI, p. 580.

[3] *Ibid.,* p. 20: «Ebbene, qual è il significato di codesta dottrina del Vico? Essa c'insegna che noi possiamo dire di conoscere un oggetto soltanto se questo oggetto non è niente di immediato: niente che il pensiero nostro trovi innanzi a sè già incominciando a conoscerlo, reale perciò prima ancora che sia conosciuto. Immediata conoscenza è *contradictio in adjecto.*»

true is the same thing as the spiritual reality which knows by realizing its act of knowing.[4]

Vico, according to Gentile, taught that we can only know an object when that object is neither found nor discovered by our thought as existing before we began to know. Vico must have seen, therefore, that knowing is resolving an object into one's own spiritual activity.[5] Truth, then, involves a making, a creative activity. In this Vico anticipated Kant and Hegel.

With regard to the Deity, Gentile aligned Vico with St. Paul and St. Augustine and their view on the presence of God in the world. Gentile states that in these men it is evident that «we have that immanence of the divine in the mind of man, which we see in the doctrine of providence of Vico.» We have already seen Gentile's position concerning St. Paul and St. Augustine and also his praise of them in Chapter II.

Another philosopher who influenced Gentile's thought on God was Baruch Spinoza. In Gentile's view Spinoza made two contributions to philosophy. Both of these came in his *Ethica.* First, Spinoza eliminated the dualism between the intellect and the will and therefore between thinking and loving.[6] Second, Spinoza insists that God knows and loves himself when man turns himself with similar act toward God.[7] Spinoza tells

[4] *Ibid.*, p. 21.

[5] *Ibid.*, pp. 20-21: «Volete sapere che cosa è una lingua ?... la lingua vera ... non è il risultato del processo linguistico, ma appunto questo processo che è sviluppo in atto. Dunque la lingua, tutto che sia realtà spirituale, e che voi conoscerete si, come s'è detto, risolvendo nella vostra attività spirituale; ma a grado a grado instaurando quella medesimezza o unità, in cui la cognizione consiste... Vero è che il fatto, con cui si converte il vero, essendo la stessa realtà spirituale che realizza (o che intende realizzando) se stessa, non è propriamente un fatto, ma un farsi. Sicche piuttosto dovrebbe dirsi: verum et fieri convertuntur.» See also footnote 2, p. 108.

[6] Baruch Spinoza, *Ethics,* Part II, Prop. 49, corollary; (tr. by Wm. H. White) in *The European Philosophers from Descartes to Nietzsche,* ed. by Monroe Beardsley, New York, 1959, p. 224.

[7] *Discorsi di religione,* p. 69: «Si ricordi Spinoza, Dio conosce ed ama d'amore intellettuale stesso nella conoscenza ed amore intellettuale onde l'uomo torna a Dio.»

us that our intellectual love for God is part of the infinite love of God for Himself. Here the dualism between God and man is abolished by the fact that «the love of God toward man and the intellectual love of the mind toward God are one and the same thing.» [8] It would seem that the two tenets of Spinoza fit very properly within Gentile's method of immanence (elimination of transcendence and dualisms) and his concept of the act of thinking as infinite and absolute. We can add that this thought of Spinoza is the theme of Gentile's ethical theory in his final work. [9] Gentile asserts that true understanding is the extension of one's concern for others and involves the reduction of external otherness to an internal other. Therefore, understanding is also love in the truest and most concrete sense.

b. *Kant and Hegel.*

As Gentile examined the philosophers of the past, he saw great contributions coming from Germany. These contributions to idealism were transmitted to Gentile through Jaja from Bertrando Spaventa. Spaventa had called for a union of Italian and German philosophy for the sake of philosophy itself. In fact Spaventa encouraged an overcoming of Italian national prejudice against all foreign philosophers. [10]

However, Gentile went to the works of Immanuel Kant and George F.W. Hegel to find encouragement for his idealistic tendencies. Spaventa had been more interested in Hegel, although he was not a blind follower. Gentile was not a blind follower of either, but rather a very critical disciple of both Kant and Hegel. In fact it would seem that, at least quantitatively speaking, his criticisms outnumbered the insights he discovered in the writings of these men. Let us now briefly examine Gentile's specific intellectual relationship with these two great German philosophers.

[8] *Op. cit.*, Part V, Prop. 36, and Corollary, p. 182.
[9] *Genesi e struttura della società*, Chapter V.
[10] B. Spaventa, *Logica e metafisica*, (9th. ed.), Bari, 1911, pp. 12-17.

Gentile thought that Kant's great contribution to philosophy was his distinction between the empirical ego and the transcendental ego as found in his *Critique of Pure Reason.* Unfortunately Kant never fully realized what he had discovered and did not follow his subjective idealism through to an actualistic idealism. [11] Nevertheless, Kant was attempting to overcome the abstractness and immediacy which was so characteristic of so many of the philosophies that had gone before him. Gentile thinks that Kant might have intended his transcendental idealism to possess an Ego like that of actual idealism but that such an attempt failed. Kant made his Ego creative of the world of subjective experience but failed to make it creative of the very same world of experience in its absolute objectivity. Even Fichte, according to Gentile, was ensnared in this subjective idealism and could not escape it. [12]

Kant made several errors if his thought is looked at from the viewpoint of actualistic idealism. His main error was to accept the world, the sensible manifold, as a datum. By doing this, he did not escape the «intellectualistic residua» of past philosophies. The content of the sensible manifold remained outside of, exterior to, independent of our thinking's true, concrete, elaborative and creative activity. Therefore, the world remains a pre-supposition of thought. Even Kant's theory on the space-time intuitions or forms doesn't save him completely from Gentile's criticism because although Gentile praises Kant's intuition that space and time are subjectivity and his «great-receptacle» theory, multiplicity remains a pre-supposition in Kant. Rather it is our mind's spatializing activity which generates multiplicity. Space and time are in us; whatever is spatial or temporal is such only because of the spatializing and temporalizing activity of the transcendental ego. [13]

Gentile also attacked the «synthetic a priori» judgment of Kant, and this not only because one part of it held to the

[11] *Teoria generale dello spirito,* pp. 6-7.

[12] *Discorsi di religione,* pp. 50-51. Gentile speaks very little of Fichte in his works.

[13] *Teoria generale dello spirito,* pp. 119-121.

data of the sensible world but because even the subjective part of it involved the categories of the understanding — and for Gentile these «categories» are merely abstractions, concepts. Each category is like a «pensiero pensato.» Then, in order to account for truly concrete experience of God, immortality and freedom, Kant had to posit the «noumenon» or the «noumenal» order. [14] Again this is an appeal to his dogmatic and metaphysical heritage in order to solve the problem of certain phenomena, and it was caused by his restrictive view of man's thinking powers.

Although Gentile did not like Kant's break-up of the unity of reason into Pure Reason and Practical Reason [15] and the replacing of true and proper cognitions with postulates (he called this a «Kantian pragmatism» because it was an attempt to unify thought and action), nevertheless, he praises Kant as well as Hume for their critiques of metaphysics (which science Gentile describes as «a philosophy of intellectual intuition»). The foregoing does not imply that Gentile did not believe that thinking had a moral aspect. He did. A man is just as responsible for what he thinks as for what he does. However, he did not believe that holding this view called for a disunification of the act of thinking. In his work on the foundations of law, [16] Gentile examined the notion of the «autonomous will» of Kant and pointed out several relationships of viewpoint with the Italian philosopher Rosmini. He did not attempt to discover an influence of Kant on Rosmini but merely made a comparative analysis of the two men's thought. Gentile's summary criticism was that neither man completely avoided intellectualistic presuppositions.

Gentile's intellectual relationship to Hegel was somewhat the same as his relationship to Kant. Hegel too approached the philosophical «vision» which Gentile was to espouse, but Hegel like Kant was not radical enough. Hegel had to be «set

[14] *Discorsi di religione*, pp. 51-52.

[15] *Teoria generale dello spirito*, pp. 77-79; see also *Sistema di logica*, I, p. 42.

[16] *I fondamenti della filosofia del diritto*, (3d ed.), Firenze, 1961, pp. 15-31.

straight,» and this involved a reform of the great insight of Hegel — his method or his dialectic. However, before we consider this «reform,» let us first of all see what Gentile thought to be noteworthy in Hegel.

Gentile felt that Hegel deserved credit for affirming the necessity of the dialectical thinking of reality in its concreteness.[17] Hegel saw that reality could not be conceived dialectically if we did not conceive reality itself as thought and distinguish the intellect which conceives things from the reason which conceives spirit or mind. If reality were to be considered intellectually, it would have to be known piecemeal, thing by thing, and each thing separate and distinct from all others. Reason, on the other hand, takes all reality within the unity of mind and sees all things as identical as well as different from others. (The theme of relations considered as internal runs throughout Gentile's works.) Hegel, therefore, was on the right track in his view of thought and its dialectical nature because within such a view thought understands itself as a unity within difference and understands things as variety within unity. One could say that the insight of «pensiero pensante» is here. Unfortunately it is hidden, buried and imprisoned.

In Gentile's opinion Hegel's forward movement toward a true idealism stopped when he began to fixate his thought with abstract concepts. In his major work on Hegel[18] Gentile tells us that the fundamental error of Hegel was his discovery of thought and reality outside the act of thinking in which thought realizes itself, i.e., «wherein (there is) the concept of the 'a priori,' the constitutive principle of experience and the realization of the pure self.»[19] This thought, Gentile tells

[17] *Teoria generale dello spirito,* pp. 54-7. One might suggest further scholarly study on the relationship between the dialectic of Gentile and Fichte rather than Gentile and Hegel. Yet Gentile did not write a «reform» of the fichtean dialectic. See also H. S. Harris, «Fichte e Gentile,» *Giornale critico della filosofia italiana,* Fasc. IV, 1964, pp. 557-578.

[18] *La riforma della dialettica hegeliana,* (2nd. ed.), Messina, 1913.

[19] *Ibid.,* p. 244.

us, was an original inspiration of Kant in his analysis of judgments. However, Hegel failed to show how his concepts of being, non-being and becoming can be unified in a real, continuous and dialectical process. To Gentile these concepts become immobile, and Hegel becomes caught up in a classic dilemma in his Logic. [20]

Let us now see how Gentile appraises Hegel's situation in the *Logic*. Hegel was trying to analyze the notion of becoming. However, he made being both identical with and different from non-being. Now this gives us a being which is not non-being and a non-being which is not being. Such a situation lacks the unity of difference which gives us becoming. What we are finally left with is two dead abstractions with no unification possible through the living movement of thinking. [21]

Hegel's thought is to be criticized here because he made his dialectic a dialectic of «thing thought» rather than a dialectic of true thinking outside of which there is no thought. Hegel was seeking real being and ended up with a being which he called an «indeterminate absolute.» If thought exists at all it is not an «indeterminate absolute,» it is act; and if we are to eliminate all the difficulties in the hegelian dialectic, we must realize that the act of true thought lies in the self-positing of reality, in becoming. Only then will we see the immense difference between thought as Plato and Aristotle conceived it, and thought as it should be conceived. Hegel did not completely avoid this error of the Greeks. Both Fichte and Hegel treated reality as a necessary presupposition of the activity which comprehends it. For these men reality is thought about. For Gentile reality is thinking. One of Gentile's followers has appraised this «reform» as a profound transformation of Hegel's union of thougth and reality. By this «reform,» Gentile reaffirmed the act of thinking as the proper life of the personality in its spirituality, and therefore this

[20] *Ibid.*, p. 55: «Celebri sono le difficoltà incontrate da lui ... nella deduzione delle prime categorie della sua *Logica*, e quindi di quel concetto del divenire, che è il carattere specifico della dialettica.»

[21] *Teoria generale dello spirito*, pp. 54-59.

reform enriches and deepens the augustinian principle of interiority. [22]

Therefore, a major difference between the two men lies in their view of Spirit. Gentile could not bring himself to objectify the spirit into an «Absolute Spirit.» If Absolute, it is as unknowable as the external world, and we have skepticism. If immanent, it loses its absoluteness and becomes dependent upon the empirical ego and, therefore, a state of mime. This leads to solipcism. The dilemna is avoided because for Gentile spirit had to be more personal, yet infinite, because it belongs to the transcendental self. However, both philosophers, Gentile and Hegel, agreed that Christianity is a spiritual religion, and that spirit is self-creative and pervades the whole of human history.

Gentile insisted that even a reality created by the spirit is not a spiritual reality if already finished and complete because then there would be no room for free activity. His actual idealism became the logical development of this principle: the activity of thinking is the only thing that is truly dialectical. Hegel did not quite arrive at this insight. [23]

### c. *Johann Fichte.*

In spite of the frequent mention of Kant and Hegel in the works of Gentile and the scarcity of references to Fichte, it is still felt that Gentile is closer in spirit to the thought of Fichte than to that of any other German idealist. [24] The affinity of the thought covers many areas of philosophy. Each phil-

[22] Armando Carlini, «Spiritualismo Assoluto e Spiritualismo Cristiano,» *Giovanni Gentile: La Vita e il Pensiero,* Vol. 8, pp. 97-123.

[23] Roger Holmes in *Idealism of Giovanni Gentile,* pp. 160-161, points out another difference between Gentile on the one hand, and Kant and Hegel on the other, namely, that for the latter two a deduction of the categories was necessary for their philosophies, whereas Genile had only one category, the act of thinking. Categories must be deduced from something, and if that something cannot be presupposed, then it can only be the self-creative act of thinking.

[24] R. W. Holmes, *op. cit.,* p. 4; H. S. Harris, «Fichte e Gentile,» *Giornale critico della filosofia italiana,* Fasc. IV, 1964, pp. 557-559.

osopher was greatly interested in the education of youth and the history of his particular State. They rejected the «noumenon» of Kant because it leads to dogmatism and is a residuum of the older metaphysics; they also wanted to found a philosophy which was free from suppositions and thus create a philosophy of freedom. Fichte, like Gentile, distinguished the transcendental and empirical egos and initiated the dialectical method which was to be used to express their thought. [25] The transcendental ego of both of them is a creative, self-determining activity. Thus the ground of experience is man's free moral activity.

Gentile himself praised Fichte for his attempt to overcome the kantian philosophy through his concept of the unity of the self and non-self and for demonstrating that «the Self cannot think another unless it thinks of itself together with the other...» [26]

However, in spite of the evident similarities the thought of the two philosophers is not identical. According to Gentile, Fichte and the other German idealists betrayed the idealist tradition because they held that the consciousness of man is affected by the external world. [27] He criticizes the admission of Fichte that consciousness does not have a first moment because the first moment is an unconscious act. [28] The Ego only becomes conscious of itself when it is shocked by the presence of the non-self. The world is somehow felt and through this act Self is first awaked to the consciousness of itself. It is this which led Hegel to conclude that Fichte never

[25] G. Gentile, *Introduzione alla filosofia*, p. 25.

[26] G. Gentile, *Le origini della filosofia contemporanea in Italia*, Firenze, 1957, p. 157: «La conquista di Fichte è quella del concetto dell'Io come unità di Io e non-Io: ossia egli ha il merito di avere approfondito il concetto kantiano della categoria, e in generale dell'apriori dell'Io stesso, mostrandone la generazione, e dimostrando che l'Io non può pensare altro, se non pensando se stesso come se stesso insieme ad altro; sintesi positiva degli opposti.» (Tr. mine.)

[27] H. S. Harris, *op. cit.*, p. 573.

[28] *Ibid.*, p. 573. Also cf. J. G. Fichte, *Grundiss des eigentumlichen der Wissenschaftslehre, Sammtliche Werke*, I (Ed. by I. H. Fichte), Berlin, 1845-46, p. 410; other works treating of God are: *On The Basis of Our Belief in a Divine Providence* (1798), *On The Definition of the Idea of Religion* (1798)

advanced beyond Kant's noumenal problem,[29] and Gentile to remark that the fichtean notion of the ego as unconscious was an admission of failure.

We should also mention that F. Copleston thinks that the God of Fichte was not immanent to each man's act of thinking through the creative activity of the transcendental ego. Fichte held that we cannot even think God since consciousness demands thinking the distinction between the ego and non-ego. In the idea of God there is no such distinction and therefore God cannot come within the act of thinking.[30] He is perhaps to be identified with a moral world order. Thus Gentile's philsophy of God would not be taken from that of Fichte.[31]

d. *Bertrando Spaventa.*

Gentile received the impetus for his hegelian reform from Spaventa. Spaventa is spoken of as a «neopolitan neo-hegelian,» but this does not mean that he was content with a mere transition of Hegel's thought. Spaventa praised in Vico what Gentile was to praise and together with Gentile criticized Vico for opposing God and nature. Spaventa saw Vico as the philosopher of history and criticized Descartes for not seeing history as a process of the spirit. He saw Vico as the precursor of the new metaphysics of mind rather than being and, therefore, the founder of the philosophy of history.[32]

Spaventa saw, with Hegel, that the spirit transforms reality, but for Spaventa the spirit is continuous development. Spirit is essentially thinking and reflection, and reality is the product of self-consciousness. When we think of something,

and *Atheismusstreit* (1799); see also *The Vocation of Man* (tr. by R. Chisholm), New York, 1956.

[29] G. F. W. HEGEL, *Logic,* (tr. by Wm. WALLACE), Oxford, 1895.

[30] F. COPLESTON, *op. cit.,* Vol. VII, Part I, p. 104.

[31] *Ibid.,* p. 104: COPLESTON states: «The idea of a subject to which nothing is opposed is thus 'the unthinkable idea of the Godhead.'» Copleston took this citation from the editions of his *Works* by his son, I. H. FICHTE, I, p. 254.

[32] B. SPAVENTA, *Logica e metafisica,* p. 23, I have not stressed the point, but it might be mentioned that for Gentile history and philosophy are identical. Past, present, the whole of reality, are resolved in the historical act.

we have already overcome the limitation which it places upon us. As sensed, it is an external thing. In the act of my knowing that I am thinking about it, it loses its externality. In any thing I think of, Spaventa tells us, «I am intimate to myself, because I identify myself — my thought — in the thing.» [33] It is not difficult to see the seeds of Gentile's actualism in these thoughts, nor in Spaventa's belief that self-consciousness does not take place in a self which is a negation of the natural self. The transcendental ego for Spaventa, just as for Gentile, does not annihilate the empirical ego. Subjectivity and objectivity are overcome in the infinite consciousness of the act of self-consciousness of our infinite and universal selves. [34]

Spaventa did not agree completely with the hegelian notion of the dialectic of being and non-being, and his criticism led Gentile to his notion of reform. This involved a reform of Hegel's concept of nothingness. Being and non-being or nothingness are but two dead abstractions. Absolutely indetermined being is unthinkable because the very thinking of it would give it determination and distinction. If non-being is thought of, it becomes identical with being. This means that act, becoming, is the prime concrete concept or thought. Being cannot be anything other than becoming. [35]

In spite of this criticism Spaventa's appreciation of Hegel was, according to Gentile, profound. Spaventa perceived the secret processes of Hegel's new intuition of the world. Spaventa saw that it was a process which is an absolute resolution of the nature into spirit, of reality into its consciousness. [36] Spaventa praised Hegel for his new «science of the spirit,» which overcame exteriority but unfortunately did not annihil-

[33] *Ibid.*, p. 128: «Lo spirito è continuo sviluppo, appunto perchè è pensiero e riflessione. Quando io penso una cosa, ho già superato la limitazione che essa in me produce. La cosa, solo percepita sensibilmente, è qualcosa di estraneo alla mia natura spirituale; nella cosa pensata io sono intimo a me stesso, perchè riconosco me stesso-il pensiero nella cosa.»

[34] *Ibid.*, pp. 128-129.

[35] G. Gentile, *Bertrando Spaventa,* Firenze, 1920, pp. 119-123.

[36] *Ibid.*, Introduction, p. X.

ate it.[37] Exteriority involves transcendency and unknowableness. Spaventa held that this was the province of the metaphysician, and therefore he was not a metaphysician. The transcendental aspect of reality which he believed in was «transcendental» in the kantian sense. Like Gentile, Spaventa sought for a unity of Kant and Hegel. He tried to resolve the kantian presupposition of the synthesis a priori which involves sameness and difference and the notion of thought in Hegel. He concluded that thought can only explain itself by prescinding from itself. Thought or thinking must be conceived as the principle of everything.[38]

Spaventa's works led Gentile toward his criticism of naturalism, mechanism and positivism. Spaventa not only encouraged Gentile's natural tendency toward idealistic philosophy but also put naturalists on the level of metaphysicians and dogmatists. Spaventa believed that the naturalism of the naturalists was «the most ferocious dogmatism that could be.» Truth and reality for naturalists lies only in the immediacy of sense observation and experience. He accused the naturalists of having tried to take over the natural sciences when this is not the function of philosophy.[39]

Spaventa's view of God is revealed in a defense of Hegel's system. Spaventa rejected the accusation that Hegel's philosophy was a political pantheism. Spaventa pointed out that the accusers were confusing pantheism with a philosophy in which God is not outside of the world but is in it, and that without the world and its phenomena (nature, people, motion, etc.), God would be nothing but an abstraction, and «essere in se.»[40] One might recall here Gentile's dictum that without man there is no God; just as there is no man without God.[41]

As we can see, the influence of Spaventa on Gentile lies not only in the foundations of the philosophy of actualistic idealism, but it extends also to the notion of God. Chiochetti

[37] *Ibid.*, p. 147.
[38] *Ibid.*, p. 153-154.
[39] *Ibid.*, p. 126.
[40] *Ibid.*, pp. 40-41.
[41] Cf. *infra*, p. 71, footnote 1.

relates a rather significant statement made by Spaventa in which he says that the «old God» of the naturalists, the transcendent God, is now dead in spite of the hopes of some that He had returned from the dead. Spaventa states that the new God is as yet an infant, known only to a few and has come into the world thanks to the philosophers of Naples and Danzig. These men, by killing the old God, also dealt the death blow to naturalism, materialism and atheism. Gentile comments that Spaventa meant that the transcendent God is dead, killed by Vico and Kant. At the same time they discovered the new God of idealism, the God who is truly immanent to men. [42]

e. *Originality of Gentile's Position.*

As we can see from the influences on Gentile, he chose the idealistic tradition as the one most in harmony with his own view of human experience. His sources were philosophical and theological, Italian and non-Italian. However, his main concern was to show that the idealist philosophers were not radical enough in their idealism. They did not carry their subjective view of experience far enough and therefore were never able to transcend completely the epistemological origins of philosophy in the Western world — the Greek tradition of

[42] Emilio CHIOCHETTI, *La Filosofia di Giovanni Gentile*, pp. 223-224. Chiochetti cites GENTILE's *La Critica*, XIII, fasc. 1, 1914, *La riforma dello hegelismo* (Bertrando SPAVENTA), II, p. 39: «Il vecchio Dio, che sebbena decollato ... non si dava per morto, rideva a crepapelle dalla consolazione: espulso dalla finestra, sperava di entrare per la magna porta dell'uomo... In apparenza egli rientrò: la ristaurazione fu festeggiata con canto e con colpi di cannone: i divoti rialzarono gli altari..., ma fu illusione ottica: erano i morti che figuravano da vivi; e in realtà era entrato il nuovo Dio, noto soltanto a pochi, ancora bambino... i cui vagiti erano coperti dal suono degli organi e delle campane. E tutto questo fracasso non fece nè anche udire l'ultimo grido del vecchio Dio, il quale era stato morto davvero; e chi gli recise il fatal capello, fu una o meglio, due persone dabbene, timorate di Dio, spiriti solitari, con parruca e codino; l'una dal golfo Napoli, l'altra da quel di Danzica. E uccidendo lui, uccisero con lo stesso colpi il naturalismo, il materialismo, l'ateismo.»

intellectualism and dualism. This vitiated their attempts at true, concrete interiority and unity of thought. Gentile showed this more specifically when entering into detailed criticism of Vico, Spinoza, Kant and Hegel, and in his more systematic elaboration of Spaventa's basic thought and notion of God, as we have seen above. We shall review below, from another aspect, what we have just seen on these men.

Gentile is also original in his approach to Christianity when rejecting its dualisms. Christianity thaught the immanence of God to man and the world; unfortunately for St. Paul and the others, this was only one side of a dualism. God had to be transcendent as well because He was infinite and Pure Act. Even mystical theology could not avoid making God an unknowable object. To Gentile this was nothing but Greek intellectualism in a religious context, using religious terms. However, as regards St. Augustine, Gentile is mostly complimentary. He seems to abstract completely from the fact that Augustine is a Catholic theologian, with everything that that means, and contents himself with the augustinian insight of the interiority of truth. This was eventually transferred by Gentile to the interiority of God.

Gentile had high praise for these basic notions but felt that his contribution to their enrichment and fulfillment was the «method of immanence.» This method, on the negative side, eliminated the problems which Christianity had faced because of its doctrine of the transcendence and ineffability of God. The distinctions and dualism we have seen fall (Chapter II) were the causes of the controversies with skeptics, agnostics, atheists, and positivists. Even Vico could not completely overcome his Catholiscism (God and nature are distinct), and therefore missed the notion of true immanence and becoming.

On the positive side, thinking replaced the God of the scholastics as the «pure act.» We see then that Gentile's novel attack on philosophy was two-pronged — the negative excision of «intellectualistic and dualistic residua» by application of the «method of immanence» and the positive affirmation of the eternal, infinite, dialectical character of each man's act of thinking. Because of his negative and positive approach, Gentile opposed himself to his entire heritage with the possible exception of his closest «formateurs» — Spaventa and Jaja. We have seen (in Chapter IV) that Descartes (and even Berkeley) made God a concept, a transcendent Being; Kant divided the unity of thinking and had to explain God by the creation of a noumenal order to replace the metaphysical which he had rejected. Therefore, Gentile had to take subjective intuitions of space, time and the categories and unify them within the human spirit as acts, not facts, or empty forms or concepts. Gentile took the hegelian Absolute and personalized it while excising any thought of dualism or pantheism. Gentile claimed to have inverted the hegelian problem with his own brand of idealism by insisting that the true philosophical problem is not a matter of drawing out thought from nature and nature from the logos; rather, nature and the logos must be deduced from actual thinking and not from thought defined abstractly. They must be brought out from thinking which is absolutely ours, thinking in which the true Self is realized. The logos of Hegel never attains to the true concept of the dialectic of pure thinking. True individuality is never discovered.[43]

From these thoughts it follows that Gentile's authentic Deity was not the Transcendent Deity of Kant, an Absolute Spirit. God is not a «noumenon» for Gentile: a «noumenon» is simply an abstraction placed in opposition to the Subject. Kant opposed intellect to will and made God a postulate of the will, an entity of the noumenal order transcendent to the will which postulates Him. By doing this, Kant vitiated his rejection of speculative or rationalistic demonstration and traditional metaphysics. Gentile pushed the kantian and berkeleyian subejectivity and augustinian interiority to its extreme. Man, who is spiritual reality, in his self-creating act creates both his intellect and his will. The creation of one is identical with the other. «The intellect is the will,» Gentile tells us, and therefore the powers of the will are not distinct from those of the intellect.[44] God, therefore, is not an Absolute Spirit, nor is He absolutely immanent to each man's true reali-

[43] *Teoria generale dello spirito,* pp. 66-67.
[44] *Ibid.,* p. 227.

ty, which is his spirit. It is within this spirit's acts of self-consciousness that He dwells if He dwells or exists at all. We can see that what Gentile did was to give a creative or generative power and unity to the Transcendental Ego which Kant did not give. Gentile's theistic metaphysics is immanentism and spiritualistic and actualistic monism carried to its ultimate degree. God is not only in man or immanent to him. He is the creation of man as man creates himself. One might call it a continuous concomitant co-creation. We have called it a «spiritualistic and actualistic monism» because the only true, concrete reality is the «realtà spirituale,» [45] the spirit of each man which is the reflective, pure act of thinking. This would seem to be the case in spite of Gentile's talk of the empirical ego, the God of the empirical ego, etc. We shall analyze this further in the final chapter.

## 2.- EVOLUTION IN GENTILE'S THOUGHT

When we speak of evolution in a philosopher's thought, we usually mean an act or process of growth or development of ideas or even a radical change of viewpoint. Often we distinguish «periods» or «stages» of this development. To some extent this latter type of distinction can be made in Gentile, but it would not be because of a radical or basic switch of philosophical position or view of reality. I submit that it would be only because of a change of emphasis.

The early stage of Gentile's philosophical career was spent mainly in the study of the past. While he studied, taught and wrote on his philosophical predecessors, [46] he was formulating his own ideas, what was to become his own system. However, it should be noted that the events in Europe in the nineteenth century and shortly after the turn of the century affected his

[45] *Ibid.*, p. 227.

[46] In this early period Gentile examined the thinkers of the past — especially Italian thinkers. His later works constantly related his own ideas to those of the past. At least twenty of his books were devoted to a critical analysis of the history of philosophy, although the criticism was not always in the light of his own thought.

thinking. The philosophy of Auguste Compte was rampant. Compte's Italian representative, Robert Ardigò, and his followers presented Gentile with an intellectual crisis — the crisis or challenge of positivism which he realized would have to be met sooner or later.[47] He met it head-on with the first systematic presentation of his new idealism. This is why Sciacca stated:

> Although actualism draws its inspirations and motivations from the successive thought of Kant, Hegel and Spaventa and the philosophy of the Renaissance from Vico, and the Risorgimento, one should not forget nonetheless, that his actualism matured through and in the crisis of positivism, which was still at its peak at the time of Gentile's intellectual formation.[48]

During these early years Gentile's disenchantment with scholastic philosophy was leading to his reaction against the Catholic Church and its rejection of his philosophy. The Church could embrace his attack on positivism but could not absorb his notion of spirit and God within its theology. The gentilian reaction led to the «method of immanence» and the reform of the past. He himself tells us that this was systematically begun in 1916 with the publication of the *Teoria generale dello spirito come atto puro,* which was the outgrowth of his lectures at the University of Pisa during the years 1915-1916. This work was followed the next year by the *Sistema di logica,* which was the result of his course in the year 1917 at the same university.[49] As we have seen, his system involved both a criticism of the past and a positive statement, which he called «actual idealism.» Benedetto Croce provided the impetus for the elucidation of various parts of the new system by posing problems to Gentile and thus causing the

[47] Robert Ardigò (1828-1920) was the leader of the positivistic movement in Italy. He left the Catholic priesthood to follow Compte's philosophy and became a professor at the University of Pisa.

[48] Michele SCIACCA, *La filosofia oggi,* Torino, 1958, p. 56 (tr. mine). This work has been translated into English by Attilio SALERNO and is entitled: *Philosophical Trends in the Contemporary World,* Notre Dame, Ind., 1964.

[49] See the prefaces to the various editions of these works.

running polemic in the *Giornale critico della filosofia italiana.* From time to time Gentile answered Croce in his major works.[50]

In the preface to the *Sistema di logica,* he tells us that the systematic exposition of his ideas was to satisfy a need which he had felt for a long time, a need to fill the abyss in the philosophy of the nineteenth century, which although modern, did not resolve the ancient problems. There was needed a reform of the kantian and hegelian insights and a refutation of positivism for this abyss to be filled. The nineteenth century had closed the door on many problems, and Gentile wishes to reopen them and keep them open. His two major expository works are intended to raise up and affirm the unity of the concrete and abstract logic in its very concreteness. Only then can the old philosophical problems even make sense.

If there is a third stage or mature period in Gentile's career, one might say that it is the application of his basic principles to a variety of problems as they occurred. I don't believe that Gentile ever wavered from his basic actualism; but he did shift his attention from one aspect or branch of philosophy to another. He had always been interested in education, and many of his ideas grew out of his thoughts on conceptual communication, the student's own thinking, etc. In fact it was the educational situation in Italy that brought out his theories. At least four of his major works were philosophico-pedagogical. This interest was rewarded by Mussolini when Gentile was appointed Minister of Education on the newly-formed Grand Fascist Council.

The political upheaval in Italy which led to the fascist victory in 1922 gave Gentile the opportunity to emphasize and stress the political thought latent in his actual idealism.[51] It

[50] *Teoria generale dello spirito,* pp. 207-209, treats of their differences concerning the philosophy of history. They also differed on the philosophy of art and mysticism. The similarities and differences in their thought are also pointed out by Nicola Monaco in his article, «La filosofia di Giovanni Gentile,» *Gregorianum,* Vol. IV (1923), pp. 432-434.

[51] The Lateran Treaty of 1929 was opposed by Gentile, and this, together with the declaration of war in Ethiopia and the military alliance with Hitler in 1939, led Gentile to question the original ideals of the Fascist Party.

also made him think on social problems, on the dialectic of the individual and the State as well as the origin and structure of society. His political works explained fascism and the relationship between fascism and culture and were published in the 1920's.

It was only years later, after his death, that the *Genesi e struttura della società* was finally published. This book, Gentile tells us in its Preface, was the development of his discussion of the State and political life made in the *Foundations of the Philosophy of Law.*[52] The *Genesis and Structure of Society* was born in the schoolroom, an outgrowth of a series of lectures given on «The Transcendental Theory of the Will and of Society.» Gentile tells us that its fourth chapter is something new to philosophy and contains a thesis which neither he nor anyone else has ever developed. The general theme of this chapter is that of the *Teoria generale dello spirito* and the «method of immanence» applied to society. Society is transcendental, it is in and comes from the inner man («in interiori homine»). Society is ideal, it is the synthesis of subject and object that arises from the immanent dialectic of the spiritual act. Actual idealism is applied to the man-State problem which Gentile had been thinking about since at least the early 1920's. Again we see this is only a matter of emphasis applied throughout his career according to the needs or crises of the time as he saw them. His writings on religion and God came about in the same way.

In the preface to the fourth edition of his *Teoria generale dello spirito,* he tells us that he has made no new substantial modification but that the third and fourth editions were intended only to give a «neatness of expression,» to «dissipate shadows» and give an «expression... more rigorous and more clear.»[53] In the middle part of his career his emphasis was put on logic and the logocentric nature of reality. Ultimately, however, the stress was being put on man because if reality is

[52] *I fondamenti della filosofia del diritto,* first published in Pisa in 1916 and again in 1923 and 1937 in Rome, was finally published by Sansoni of Firenze in 1961.

[53] *Teoria generale dello spirito,* Prefazione, pp. v-vii.

spiritual, it is in man that the spirit or spiritual act is found. Man takes on infinite value. Therefore we might say that a definite humanism runs concomitantly with logocentricity. There is no thinking without man, and man would be only a thing, a completion but for his act of thinking. Man's thinking is moral because he is responsible for what he thinks; it is creative and not just an intellectual process. Loving and understanding become one. Gentile's humanism, his love of mankind, is very evident in his works on education, law, the State and Society, and even religion, since we saw in Chapter II that he does not like the idea of a mysticism which reduces man to nothingness.[54] For this reason one might also call his philosophy a «humanistic idealism.»[55]

[54] *Discorsi di religione.* In its preface, he tells us he is writing a second edition in order to bring his thought on religion up to date in the light of the many things that had happened to Italy between 1920 and 1924. The 1934 edition was intended to put his thought in systematic form.

[55] One author calls it an «actual humanism:» H. S. Harris, *The Social Philosophy of Giovanni Gentile,* Urbana, Ill., 1960, Chapter 3. It is interesting to note the similarities between the careers and interests of Gentile in Italy and John Dewey in America. Both witnessed great changes in their countries, both were influenced by Hegel and each man applied his speculative mind to educational and social problems.

# CHAPTER VI

## THE VALUE OF GENTILE'S POSITION

The purpose of this chapter is to review the meanings that are embodied within Gentile's thought on the problem of God and, if possible, to come to sound, decisive, evaluational judgments on that thought. While there are several weaknesses inherent in his system, taken as a whole, it is not without value.

### 1.- VALUABLE ASPECTS OF GENTILE'S SYSTEM

On the whole Gentile is clear, but this clarity is somewhat limited. His sentences are often very lengthy and rambling, and at times he does not seem to address himself to the «title» of his paragraph. The reader is left waiting for something that does not come. However, whatever vagueness this may cause is compensated for by the constant repetition of his basic thought expressed in different ways. Gentile's students considered him to be an excellent teacher. The mode of expression in his books is probably the result of writing according to the flow of thoughts as they came, with the proper inflections, in the classroom. However, when all factors are considered, the average philosophy student capable of reading Italian should grasp his main positions.

Another valuable aspect lies in the fact that Gentile's thought is systematic. Certain basic logical and metaphysical principles are established and consistently applied to the various problems that fall within human philosophical experience. Abstracting from the question of the validity of these principles, we find it to be a fact that they are the consistent basis of a truly comprehensive system. Basically Gentile's philosophy is a union of thought and being; the traditional branches of epistemology, psychology and metaphysics' are brought together in his emphasis on human spirituality as revealed in the pure act of thinking. His love for metaphysics and the continuity of his thought with that of Italian Idealism is evident throughout his writings.[1] Gentile went on to address himself to the problems of God's existence, the nature of religion, man and society, morality, immorality, a philosophy of art, and an educational philosophy. Besides this effort he applied his basic thought to all of the major philosophies of the past and criticized them in the light of that thought. Gentile constantly asserted his opposition to the positivistic thinking which had been prevalent in Italy for many years. Therefore we can see that he covered all the areas of philosophical study from logic to ethics and commented on the history of philosophy as well.

A concomitant value here lies in the fact that he never changed his basic position or method. From the time of *Il modernismo* (1909) to *Genesi e struttura della società* (1943), he never wavered from his theory that the activity of human thinking or self-consciousness has a creative aspect and that the approach to philosophical problems should be dialectical.

Let us now briefly enumerate other valuable aspects of his system as a whole and then the valuable aspects of his thought on God. Taking his system as a whole, we may praise the following: the consciousness or awareness of self is a valid philosophical point of departure. This consciousness when reflecting makes us aware of the human spirit and man's freedom from the mechanistic determination of physico-chemical laws. The problem of truth may be solved by the fact that the knowledge of the transcendental ego is «mediate.» Gentile's mediacy is acceptable in the sense that there is nothing really external to the act of thinking because thinking interiorizes the object of my thought and becomes a product of the infinite self. «Other» becomes only a moment of the dialectic of thinking. There is no problem of knowing things other than

[1] As evidence of this one might consult the already mentioned word of Sciacca and also: *Contemporary Thought of Italy* (New York), 1926) by Angelo Crespi.

ourselves, which Gentile calls «immediate» knowing. Man, transcendentally considered, is spirit and «infinite,» he is the image of God on earth. Gentile's idealism does not reach the extreme of solipcism because he recognizes the existence of other minds and even the finite self of man. However, he holds that the finite and physical is unimportant. It is the infinite and spiritual aspect of man that is important.

Man's true reality is a spiritual one. He is the most God-like being in the world and, therefore, of infinite value and dignity.

Turning to other valuable aspects of Gentile's philosophy of God, we can include the following: Gentile uses the term God (Dio) and not Absolute or Unknown, or some other term which is vague and uncommon; Gentile believes in the transcendent God who is the Creator of the universe; Gentile tells us that God is a «person» and that He is «absolute:» the transcendent God becomes real for individual men by being brought within the thinking ego and is thus known, loved, willed and «created» in the single unified act of thinking. He becomes immanent and subjectively meaningful through this «creative act» [2] If men could accept Gentile's idealism, atheism would become absurd; Gentile accepts Christianity because it is a religion of the spirit and rejects pantheism because it denies the distinction between God and the world. Thus the transcendence of God is saved because of Gentile's recognition of the finite self and the finitude of nature. At the same time, divine immanence is realized through the activity of the transcendental ego. The objectivity of God is overcome, and dogmatic and mystical theology are overcome by the philosophical synthesis of the «pensiero pensante.»

However, there are basic deficiencies in his system and we shall now consider them.

## 2.- DEFICIENCES WITHIN GENTILE'S SYSTEM

In spite of the fact that Gentile has made definite contributions to philosophy and given succeeding generations of

[2] Our thinking does not create God entitatively. Cf. *supra*, p. 53.

philosophers a great deal to think about, his system and method present certain difficulties. These difficulties can be reduced to the following groups: a) Monistic tendencies in Gentile's system. b) Lack of basis in human experience. c) Doubtful meaning of the Transcendent God. d) Doubtful meaning of God's Personality.

a. *Monistic Tendencies.*

Self-consciousness is the starting point for Gentile's actualistic idealism. It is a necessary antecedent condition to all further developments in his thought. Gentile does not accept the world, God, the State as antecedent to thought to be an authentic approach, but in order to take such a monistic step, he had to posit the transcendental ego and oppose it to the empirical ego. Without this distinction his system has no base. It becomes either a confused realism or a solipcism. It would therefore seem that this distinction of «selves» is a necessary antecedent to his resolution of philosophy's perennial problems. It should also be noted that the appeal to such a distinction was made in order to resolve all dualisms. This would indicate the presupposition that a dualism is an intrinsic philosophical evil. A renowned American philosopher, William P. Montague, has commented on this distinction:

> The *supposition* that each of us possesses as the core of his nature a wonderful timeless and spaceless ego is necessitated by the dialectic of subjectivism, but nothing else whatsoever. We may look into our natures as carefully and as sympathetically as we choose without discovering anything other than the more or less helpless and commonplace self with which we are familiar.[3]

Gentile's pure ego is very like to the intellectual intuition of Fichte, who held that every act of objectification presupposes the pure ego and can therefore be called the transcend-

[3] Wm. P. Montague, *The Ways of Knowing*, London, 1925, p. 286.

ental ego. In his *History of Philosophy* Frederick Copleston relates that Fichte once said to his students:

> 'Gentlemen think the wall.' He then proceeded: 'Gentlemen, think him who thought the wall.' Clearly, we could proceed indefinitely in this fashion. 'Gentlemen, think him who thought who thought the wall,' and so on. In other words, however hard we may try to objectify the self, that is, to burn it into an object of consciousness, there always remains an I or ego which transcends objectification and is itself the condition of all objectifiability and the condition of the unty of consciousness. And it is this pure or transcendental ego which is the first principle of philosophy. [4]

The difference between the thought of many philosophers and that of Gentile would seem to lie in the fact that many make self-consciousness a reflective power of the human spirit or self; a power which recognizes man's finite condition. Gentile makes it a «creative,» transcendental self within the empirical self. In fact, he creates an apparent dualism since the activities of the empirical self have no validity apart from the transcendental self.

As a criticism of this point of Gentile's thought, we may note that the important factor here is not only whether Genile is right or wrong, justified or unjustified, but also whether or not he had posited certain conditions and demanded their acceptance before addressing himself to man's «transcendental ego.» Moreover, the transcendental ego introduced by' Gentile seems to be rather a possible logical structure than an existential reality. [5]

Perhaps the transcendent God-Creator could be substituted for Gentile's creative ego. Thus the confusion in Gentile's system between transcendental and empirical egos would be eliminated. Furthermore, Gentile's monistic tendency toward unifying everything in one transcendental ego led to a rejection of first principles as valid or meaningful in themselves, apart

[4] Frederick Copleston, *A History of Philosophy*, Vol. 7, Part 1, p. 60.
[5] Cf. *supra, Chapter* I, pp. 17-20.

from a dialectic in which the principle of excluded middle is pronounced as a synthesis. The immediacy of human experience is replaced by the transcendental activity of «mediacy.» The free creativity of the human spirit practically eliminates the possibility of authentic error.

A contemporary commentator, Michele Sciacca, in spite of his admiration of Gentile's philosophical effort, finds great difficulty in accepting Gentile's notion of «spirit» and «pensiero pensante.» He finds that Gentile reduces spirit to and identifies it with the act of logical or reflective thought. Actuality is spirit and makes itself in an eternal becoming. As such, it is never complete. Therefore, the spirit of man never attains its full actuality; the full actuality of thought will never be a reality and so it is non-reality — «but if in its fullness thought escapes itself, then thought is not immanence but an irreductible transcendence: thought always pursues itself but does not catch up with itself.» [6] Sciacca concludes that this eternal self-making is everything and nothing at the same time, «it remains immersed in its own act, a prisoner of its own exactitude, and therefore ineffable. [7]

Sciacca also points out that self-consciousness, which constantly escapes itself, posits itself as a «problem.» Thus it transcends itself. «As absolute interiority, self-conciousness is self-transcendence.» In the light of this insight we might say that God, whom Gentile tells us comes within our thought because of the creative activity of thinking, is constantly escaping full and absolute interiorization. Like self-consciousness, He is always posited as a problem and thus constantly transcends our thinking. Nevertheless, it would seem that Carlini is still correct when he says that Gentile's idea of transcendence is a transcendence rooted in immanence be-

[6] M. Sciacca, *La filosofia oggi,* Milano, 1958, p. 80: «... ma se la pianezza di se stesso sfugge al pensiero, il pensare non e immanenza, ma irriducibile trascendenza; il pensiero s'insegue sempre senza raggiungersi mai.» (Tr. mine.) See also the translation of this work by Attilio Salerno: *Philosophical Trends in the Contemporary World,* Notre Dame, Ind., 1964, especially pp. 55-62.

[7] *Ibid.*, p. 81: «Esso resta immerso nel suo atto, prigioniero della propria puntualità e percio ineffabile.» (Tr. mine.)

cause the transcendence of which Sciacca speaks stems from the problematic nature of actualistic thought itself.

Gentile also wanted to avoid mysticism, but his presupposition of the eternity of the act of thinking makes thinking a timeless instant and so leads him into mysticism, since one feels absolute in each act of thought.

Many of his contemporaries took Gentile to task for his distinction of the «egos» and his «method of immanence.» Typical of this criticism is that of the neo-scholastic philosopher, N. Balthasar. Balthasar rejected the «creative» idea of the transcendental self and insisted that our self-conscious activity was only a participation of divine thought, indirectly known; he also rejected the unity of intellect and will in man (which Gentile upheld) and re-affirmed such a unity to exist in God alone. Balthasar re-affirmed the neo-scholastic position that only God is eternal, infinite and unchanging, both in His Being and in His end. [8]

Other neo-scholastic philosophers, those from the Roman universities, also attacked the foundations and conclusions of Gentile's system. A Dominican, N. Cordovani, asserted that the gentilian idealism was an inept solution to the «critical problem,» and that by identifying reality with the act of cognition in man, Gentile was led to a «humanistic panlogism.» [9] Materialism and positivism are not truly overcome because of the lack of the acceptance of the transcendent God and the denial of the possibility of supernatural Revelation. [10]

Cordovani admits that scholastic philosophy can accept an intentional identity between thought and reality, but not a real or physical identity such as one finds in actualistic idealism. He states: «The act of the intellect is other than that

[8] N. Balthasar, «La filosofia dell'arte,» *Revue Néo-Scholastique de Philosophie de Louvain* (Vol. XXXIV), 1932, pp. 96-97: «En Dieu seul il n'y a aucune distinction réelle entre l'intelligence et la volonté, aucun progres dans l'être, aucune déviation possible de la fin dernière.»

[9] N. Cordovani, «Actualismus Italicus et realismus S. Thomae,» *Angelicum* (Annus VIII), Fasc. 4, Oct.-Nov.-Dec., 1931, pp. 515-526.

[10] *Ibid.*, p. 516: «Non est ergo minus materialisticus quam positivismus... negat Dei transcendentiam et possibilitatem revelationis supernaturalis...».

which is expressed in the idea or asserted in the judgment» and its knowledge comes from things and is about things.[11] He feels, and correctly I think, that Gentile has caused a great deal of confusion here. There is no reason why the scholastic notion should lead to skepticism as Gentile insists because «by the operation of philosophic reflection... all the elements of cognition are able to be examined...»[12]

Cordovani finishes his criticism by declaring that «this reduction of philosophy to logic, the identification of God with the transcendental ego and identification of the natural order with the supernatural is the worst abstractionism so far encountered.»[13] The ultimate result could only be the elimination of the worship of the true God, a worship which is due only to Him, because of Who and What He is.

Another neo-scholastic philosopher, Nicola Monaco, S.J., directed his attack at the foundation of Gentile's system also.[14] He addressed himself to Gentile's method which insists, as we have seen in the first chapter, that nothing can be presupposed to thought in act because the being of the spirit is nothing other than actuality. Monaco pointed out that Gentile does nothing but constantly assert the reality of the «pensiero pensante» and its pure actuality and that to Gentile it is simply evident that any explanation demands and presupposes the spiritual thinking activity. Therefore, it cannot be denied.

Monaco believed that the scholastic realists could easily match Gentile dogma for dogma (or presupposition for presupposition). The scholastics held that: «... the to-be of the spirit is a reality distinct from the effect which it produces:

[11] *Ibid.*, p. 521: «Ipse actus intellectus est aliud a re quae in idea et judicio exprimitur et asseritur; idea est conceptus facultatis ab objecto fecundatae, ita ut veritas sit in intellectu, e rebus tamen et de rebus.» (Tr. mine.)

[12] *Ibid.*, p. 521: «...ope reflexionis philosophicae... omnia elementa subjici possint.» (Tr. mine.)

[13] *Ibid.*, p. 525: «Est adhuc pessimus abstractismus ista reductio omnis philosophiae ad logicam, identitas inter Deum et ego transcendentale, inter ordinem naturalem et supernaturalem.» (Tr. mine.)

[14] Nicola Monaco, «La filosofia di Giovanni Gentile,» *Gregorianum*, Vol. IV (1923), pp. 431-464 and 517-556.

and the to-be of thought presupposes the real object as a term to which it refers and of which it is ... an ideal reproduction, a representation. And thus we may justifiably reject the gentilian assertion, declaring it to be false and opposed to the common sense of men...» [15]

Monaco accepts the assertion of «pensiero in atto» and «spirito assoluto,» etc., provided such attributes are applied to God, not to the transcendental ego: he accepts them if applied to the inner Trinitarian life, not to the finite life of man. Monaco holds that these attributes belong to God alone «outside of Whom there is only non-being, and in Whom there is every being.» [16]

Monaco's main objection to Gentile's method lies in what he calls an «equivocation». Gentile identifies being and operation, actuality and activity. In fact, Gentile reduces being to operation and activity. Gentile vitiates the principle of Vico (verum et factum convertuntur) which is a scholastic principle. Gentile fails to distinguish the one who operates from his operation, the thinker from his thought. The one is the passage from potency to act, the other is the act itself. The real perfection of any activity does not lie in the activity itself but in its term. [17]

Monaco concludes that the source of the confusion caused by Gentile lies in his language and especially the use of the term «pure act». The «authentic pure act» is that of scholastic philosophy which «is an act which always is, but never

[15] *Ibid.*, p. 457: «... l'essere dello spirito è una realtà distinta d'all'effetto che produce: e l'essere del pensiero presuppone l'oggetto reale, come termine a cui si riferisco di cui è... una riproduzione ideale, una rappresentazione. E così con pieno diritto potremmo rigettare l'asserto gentiliano, dichiarandolo falso e opposto sia al senso commune degli uomini...» (Tr. mine.)

[16] *Ibid.*, p. 457: «...fuori di cui non v'e che il non-essere, e in cui solo e ogni essere.» (Tr. mine.)

[17] *Ibid.*, p. 460: «In ogni attività e anche in quella del pensiero, convien distinguere sempre l'operazione e l'operato, che nel pensiero è la cogitatio e il cogitatum: l'una è il passagio o moto della potenza all'atto, l'altro è l'atto stesso, termine di quel moto. Ora e chiaro che la perfezione propria dell'attivita non sta nel passagio o moto, che è appunto il divenire, ma nell'atto che nè è il termine.»

becoming; whereas the gentilian pure act is an act that is always becoming but never is.» [18]

We might conclude this section by remarking that even if the traditional demonstrations for God's existence are invalid, it is doubtful that their invalidity stems from their disagreement with Gentile's logocentricity. Gentile makes God meaningful and real only for the individual, he does not make Him to be. This will be further confirmed later in the chapter. Let us examine the validity of the sources of Gentile's first principles or intuitions.

b. *Lack of a Sure Basis in Human Experience.*

It is sometimes suggested that a criticism of idealism should involve stronger insistence on the meaning and validity of common sense experience. However, Gentile considered the experience of common sense as the naive man's realism. This man is spiritually and reflectively blind. For Gentile the discovery of the true life of the spirit is the task of the philosopher who by profession must be introspective and analytical.

Nevertheless, Gentile has rejected the experience of many philosophers, even those whose tendencies are idealistic. It is this fact which makes some of his basic judgments questionable. Although there is no specific statement to which one can refer there is a phenomenon which seems to pervade Gentile's works on God. One detects an air of surprise that so many philosophers whose judgments were warped (according to Gentile) by the intellectualistic residue of ancient Greece arrived at the same conclusions as actual idealism. Gentile seemed to feel that it was simply by happy accident that some arrived at theism, but that if all had shared his insights, none would have arrived at atheism.

The gentilian experience was not that man is a union of body and soul (although he uses the term soul at times) but

[18] *Ibid.*, p. 464: «... è un atto che sempre è, nè mai diveni mentre l'atto puro gentiliano è un atto che è sempre divenire, ne mai e.» (Tr. mine.)

rather a union of two selves.[19] The empirical self is experienced as incorporated or taken within the transcedental self. Such a theory, as we say, caused a philosopher like William P. Montague, an American realist, to query the gentilian experience.[20] Do we actually experience two selves? Even if the transcendental ego is real, is it evident to man? Do we really experience ourselves as infinite, absolute, and timeless, or are we not more conscious of our limitations and our existential contingency? Do things, even thoughts, lose their meaningfulness simply because we recognize them as «other?» Can thinking lead only to new acts of thinking? Do we never experience the conceptual order of being? Cannot thoughts and judgments be actual in the sense of completed or even in the sense of being instruments for further thinking, for further problem solving?

Until such time as most philosophers, both professional and non-professional can share their basic experience with Gentile and answer the above questions in a gentilian manner, it is doubtfull that actualism represents the ultimate refutation of atheism or agnosticism.

### c. *Doubtful Meaning of «Transcendent God.»*

The implications of transcendence were not lost on Gentile. As we have seen, he did not deny the reality of the transcendent God,[21] but only the meaningfulness or authenticity of God considered as transcendent. It was his intention to show the idealistic contribution which could be made to the problem of God. God must be considered as within man, but not immanent because His conserving power extends to man. God considered from this point of view always remains exterior; even though He be a concept, He remains exterior. For Gentile God should be a creation of the Self inasmuch as it *is* spirit, inasmuch as it constantly transcends itself by a process of self-

[19] Cf. *supra*, Chapter VI, pp. 108-9
[20] *Loc. cit.*
[21] Cf. *supra*, Chapter III, p. 53.

consciousness. By disengaging himself from his empirical individuality, each man attempts to identify himself with the Absolute.[22] When this is accomplished, there is no further need of the notion of a transcendent God.'

The consequences of such a view are many — even for Gentile's own system. One may ask: can Gentile treat man in an authentic manner if he weakens the Creator-creature relationship? Is creaturehood not one of the most basic metaphysical aspects of man?

It would seem that since Gentile grants God's creative act, then God, for Gentile, ought to be the foundation of man completely considered. Consequently, God should be the foundation and cause of the transcendental ego as well as the empirical self. It is true that we can find some of these ideas in Gentile but they require serious clarification of the problem as to how God creates the transcendental ego and yet the transcendental ego creates God. Gentile clearly states that God is the foundation of man. Therefore He must be the foundation of the act of self-consciousness within which God Himself is not re-created but «created» by thinking's act of self-synthesis.[23] Since God is the foundation of our being, the transcendental ego should be a creature, but not a creator. Otherwise we have an evident pantheism which, on the other hand, Gentile wanted to avoid. Perhaps Gentile is saved when he

[22] A similar thought is expressed by Eduard Babois in his review of Gentile's book *Genesi e struttura della società* for the *Revue Philosophique de Louvain* (1955), pp. 442-3; «...cette individualité matérielle, extrinsèque en un sens, l'homme doit la transcender en la spiritualisant, pour constituer ainsi son individualité spirituelle, tout intérieure, c'est-à-dire sa personalité morale, qui doit être sa manière a lui de participer au moi absolu... .»

[23] Gentile never speaks of a «re-creation» of God by the human intellect. The intellect only produces completed thuoghts. Gentile always speaks of the act of thinking or human spirit as «creative» of reality because creative of itself. See: *Discorsi di religione*, pp. 35 and 141; also *Genesis and Structure of Society*, p. 108 and *Sistema di logica*, Vol. 1, p. 34: «Alla conoscenza intellectualistica contemplativa, che era ad Aristotele la cima più alta dell'-ascensione spirituale, sottentra una conoscenza nuova, attiva, operosa, creatrice del suo oggetto, cioè di se medesima nel suo creatrice spirituale valore.»

says that we can keep God as transcedent as we want. (Thinking and willing are one and the same.) But in such a case one would have to accept degrees of transcendence and immanence according to individual preferences. This would lead, in the last resort, to complete subjectivity and relativism. We may add that the notion of God as Creator is almost completely ignored in Gentile's philosophy.

Gentile's seeming inability to understand the metaphysical principle of causality is surprising. As we saw above in the fourth chapter his notion of the principle was rather limited. It is understandable that if he believed that cause and effect are ultimately identical, then one must grant him a pantheistic result. Gentile seems to have missed the inference that the use of this metaphysical principle together with certain evident facts taken from the physical world is based on our deepest conviction; moreover, this results in the conclusion that God is transcendent or distinct from the world because it must be of His very essence to be, whereas essence and existence are contingent in every finite entity. Gentile would not agree with much of this reasoning, but it is this position which he should have attacked more clearly and convincingly.

### d. *Ambiguity in the Notion of God as Person.*

A study of Gentile's works does not clearly reveal the personality of God. For Gentile man is a person because he is free. He is free because he is a spirit. Because he is spirit, he creates truth within himself. Therefore, Gentile speaks of truth as having a divine character and of truth as person — the divine character of truth is Person. [24] God is Truth, therefore, God must be a Person. Gentile states this categorically when he says that God is «infinite and absolute person.» However, he is vague as to the meaning of «person.» [25] Can the personality of God be distinct from that of man transcendent-

[24] *Introduzione alla filosofia*, pp. 201-202. Gentile uses the terms «persona» and «personalità.»

[25] *Ibid.*, p. 200.

ally considered? Is God a self-subsisting intelligent Being? Or is God to be identified with the «pensiero pensante» or the transcendental ego? If we make such an identification then each person is the «Person» of God, and this renders the independently subsisting rationality of God doubtful.

The confusion grows when we examine the notion of Jesus and the State, keeping in mind that Gentile considered himself to be a Christian and even a Catholic Christian. Is Jesus God ? Is the State God ? Jesus is but one person. Gentile at times speaks of Jesus as divine and at times as one who merely speaks for God. [26] He does not resolve this distinction. Of course he may mean that there is a distinction of egos in Jesus, the God-like and the infinite. Traditional theology speaks of two natures in Christ, the divine and the human. Gentile's egos would seem to pertain to Jesus more than to any other person. Unfortunately this does not come through very clearly. If Jesus is the humanized God, would He not be merely an object, a fact, for actual idealism.

Is God the State? Here again there is room for confusion because Gentile calls Fascism a religion. The Fascist State is ethical and spiritual. The State is an object which exists before empirical man and legislates for him. The Law of the State shares the divine nature because of its unchanging rigidity. The State is like the transcendent God because it exists immediately «before our eyes;» like the system of nature its laws are necessary, conceived and promulgated with an iron logic. Nevertheless this objectivity is finally resolved by the State's returning from the objective moment to philosophical authenticity through the instrumentality of the act of thinking. Since it is worth repeating, let us see again a major statement from Gentile:

> As an ethical institution in the full sense, the State returns again from objective divinity to the infinite divine spark in the heart of the subject, the point at which the universe has its center. [27]

[26] Cf. *supra*, Chapter II, sect. 4.
[27] Cf. *supra* Chapter II, pp. 42-43.

Therefore, whatever there is of the divine in man subsumes the State within itself and divinizes it just as it undoubtedly divinizes Jesus by thinking on Him and thinking on its thinking of Him.[28] If we ask again: what or who is God? the answer could again be: He is whatever or whoever we want Him to be — Nature and its inexorable laws, the State or its laws, Jesus Christ, or perhaps Mankind as represented by its individual spiritual representatives. A case could be made for each, and therefore the substantial, self-subsisting, rational existence of God is weakly considered and remains as hidden and doubtful for the gentilian idealists as it does for the mysticism which Gentile attacked.

### 3.- EVALUATION OF THE ARGUMENTS FOR THE EXISTENCE OF GOD

When speaking of arguments for God's existence we must keep in mind what we said about the notion of God. Gentile's concept seems to lead to a pantheistic or exaggerated immanence raher than a transcendent notion. Whatever the theist's reason might be for accepting one argument rather than another, many theists should find great affinity with the thought of Gentile. Throughout his works Gentile speaks as if he accepts God as a tenet of his Christian faith and the universal opinion of mankind. He uses the approach of «feeling.» Man feels a need for God in order to explain his own finite condition and in order to explain the intricate system of physical law in nature.

Gentile's approach would also appeal to anyone who can accept his concept of man, the overcoming of abstract logic, the mediacy of knowledge and therefore, the transcendental self. Therefore, in a sense, the problem of whether or not God actually exists is transformed into the problem of what God means for each man. The God who is synthesized in each man's act of thinking, is each man's God and each man's truth.

[28] The State and Jesus, like any external objects, are abstractions until made the objective moments of the act of thinking, which is the manifestation of the divine in man. External reality receives its concreteness from the activity of the transcendental ego. Cf. *supra,* Chapter I, pp. 17-18.

He is a creation of each man's spirit. The transcendent, objective God of traditional belief is brought within the subject by thinking which is never objectified because it is always becoming. Purely empirical or «a posteriori» arguments are given the subjective complement they need.

The argument for God which was presented as the third argument in the third chapter comes closest to fulfilling any objective demands concerning God's existence and nature. There we saw that God is the foundation of the orderly system of laws in nature. One may assume that this creative act demanded intelligence and awareness. Perhaps this is why Gentile says that God is a «Person.»

However, a difficulty is present as was pointed out in the footnote to the argument. The difficulty arises for anyone seeking a purely empirical point of departure and a really objective conclusion. If one re-reads the statements above on page 55, one finds Gentile saying that God can be found within our hearts or souls; and in the statements on p. 78, he says that the modern philosopher does not simply observe the world, but goes back within himself; when he knows the world (with its systems), he knows it «with his own feelings.»

In order to give a final answer to the problem raised in the footnote, I feel a further clarification is necessary. In rejecting St. Thomas' «five ways,» Gentile states that they only utilize an immediate contact with nature, and therefore God is not demonstrated. Evidently then, an immediate contact does not demonstrate God. One's own feelings of the inner presence of God in the «soul» must accompany the grasp of God in the world. Feeling replaces the reasoning process. Otherwise one «looks for God... outside of himself,» and this leads us into transcendence and immediacy. Thus we have the fusion of the subjective and objective approaches and God is reached in a truly modern philosophical manner.

This however, may lead to a very subjective and at times a false concept of God. Yet one can agree that the reason for the persistent religious thought in the history of mankind is based on a kind of feeling of God. Therefore, Gentile's argument based on feeling has its own great objective value.

## 4.- GENTILE'S CHRISTIANITY

Can Gentile truly be called a Christian? Let us first of all remember that Gentile wanted to be considered a Christian and a Catholic. Christianity was the religion of the spirit as was actualistic idealism. Gentile himself answers the question when he says: «A Christian? If by Christianity one means a religion of the humanity of God or the divine redemption of man through a spirit considered as an activity which overcomes and negates nature and which in no conceivable way could have come from nature, I have such a presumption [29]...»

However, Gentile's desire to be considered a true Christian entails serious difficulties. Among these would be the following:

1) As we saw in the second chapter, the divinity of Jesus is not clearly and concisely stated; nor is the notion of Jesus as the Redeemer of all mankind. The redemption of mankind did not come through the pure activity of the spirit, the «pensiero pensante,» which seems to be the implication of the above statement. Redemption came through Jesus Christ, Who is the Second Person of the Blessed Trinity. Gentile's appreciation of the Personality of Jesus is quite vague, as is His appreciation of Christ's redemptive mission.

2) Gentle's notion of immanence tends toward an identification of God with the spiritual activity of each man. The fact of transcendence of the immanent God is very weakly presented in his system. Thus the exaggerated theory of immanence has led to the accusations of spiritualistic monism, pantheism and atheism. The accusations are unjustified, but there is justification for the confusion.

3) Gentile's thought on immortality and the objective reality of the other world is not completely clear. One could argue that the supernatural realm is but an aspect or dimension of the act of thinking. [30] Thus even though he cites the

[29] *Introduzione alla filosofia*, p. 254.

[30] One may consult Chapter XIII of *Genesi e struttura della società* and draw his own conclusions in the light of Gentile's entire system.

Scriptures, their true worth is placed in doubt because of their transcendent aspect and source. In the spirit of Hegel Gentile makes religion, its object (God) and His revelation only a moment of the synthesis which is philosophy.

4) This brings us to the final remark. Philosophy, and specifically actualistic idealism, may pose a definite threat to the ultimate source of truth for the Christian, God's Revelation. Consequently, it undermines truth connected with divine revelation such as the teaching magisterium of the Church — the Church of which Gentile claims to be a member. The final implication would be that one's subjective knowledge is given a higher place as a source of objecive truth than any other source of divine revelation.

For these reasons I think that we can understand the fact that Gentile's own mode of Christianity was unacceptable in traditional circles. His belief in God and the spirituality of man did not save him from condemnation. [31]

[31] All of Gentile's works were placed on the Index of Forbidden Books by a decree of the Holy Office, June 20, 1934. See M. S. Sciacca, «Giovanni Gentile,» *Enciclopedia Cattolica,* Vol. VI, 1951, pp. 32-36.

# CONCLUSION

The primary conclusion of our study is that Gentile is a theist, a believer in the reality of God, albeit a theist in his own sense. This is evident not only from the many texts cited throughout this work but from two other phenomena as well. Gentile felt it necessary to demonstrate the existence of God in a positive manner and to mount an attack on the major traditional demonstrations as well. The attack, however, was not that of an atheist. Its ultimate aim was to make the way clear for a true, philosophical approach to the recognition of God as real. This extensive negative effort, which we examined in Chapter IV, was meant to be an aid to the theistic hypothesis, not a hindrance. The demonstrations which we saw in Chapter III were his positive contribution to the philosophy of God.

Not only did he try to aid «the cause» of God, but he constantly insisted that his spiritualistic metaphysics was an answer to the materialism, positivism and naturalism whch were rampant throughout Italy as well as the whole of Europe. He insisted that this spiritualistic view of man was the foundation of his creative freedom and therefore released him from the fetters of religious dogmatism and the worship of a transcendent God. The «playing down» of the traditional notion of God would make God real and important in the lives of all men. Unfortunately, the extent to which actualism accomplished this ideal has never been assessed.

This attempt to make God become real, important and authentic within thinking or self-consciousness also had the unfortunate consequence of bringing the charge of agnosticism (and therefore condemnation) from the neo-scholastic philosophers and theologians of his own day. They felt that while immanence must be maintained, Gentile's «immanence» was exaggerated. It is evident that a less careful reading of Gentile could lead to the belief that man is the true, authentic divinity and that «God» is a name which represents a human creation. This is, as we have seen repeatedly, a mistaken view, although the mistake is understandable.

There is one criticism I would make of the articles by the neo-scholastic authors mentioned in the last chapter. It is that besides the fact that they only reaffirmed the principles of thomistic realism (as worthy as they may be), they completely ignored Gentile's recognition of the empirical self and its transcendent God. They ignored the distinction between the «selves» in man. Yet Gentile's whole life, filled with outgoing activity, shows that he actually lived this distinction, and it is only this distinction which saves him from a theory of absolute immanentism.

However, in all fairness to these critics it should be pointed out that they were attempting to defuse what they considered to be a potentially dangerous theistic and religious position Their exaggerations, like Gentile's, were very likely indulged in for their polemical effect. It might also be noted that the ecumenical spirit of post-Vatican II did not pervade these controversies.

In concluding this section let it be reasserted that Gentile does not identify man and God. He only seems to do so. The transcendent God exists. Gentile himself denies that he is a pantheist when he states: «Pantheist, no, unless it is the pantheism which is Christianity itself. Pantheism denies the distinction between God and the world, and I do not deny it. [1]»

It might be noted that although Gentile disclaims pantheism, his thought lacks a developed doctrine of «participation of being.» Nevertheless, as we have seen, he often comes back to his basic belief in the spirit of man, the notion of thought thinking on itself, and therefore, the idea of our divine humanity, of man as the «imago Dei.» While he does not use the term «participation» in the infinite Being and life of God, the

[1] *Introduzione alla filosofia*, p. 205 and p. 254: «Panteista, no, se non è panteismo lo stesso cristianesimo. Il panteismo nega la distinzione, e io non la nego.»

spirit of the traditional scholastic notion is present in his thought as it pertains to man.

However, the belief in a transcendent God is of minor importance to Gentile. God must be philosophically and authentically considered. He must be approached from an entirely new position, a position which even goes beyond that of Kant and Hegel and it is this which brought on the accusation of atheism.[2] Gentile, however, did not feel that such an accusation was justified because he felt that his approach saved theism for posterity. His critics seem to have reasoned that rather than saving God and religion, actualistic idealism tended to replace them, actualistic idealism becoming the new religion and God and man brought together in the transcendental ego. In one sense they were correct. Gentile certainly gives the impression that there are several «Gods.» Besides the «Gods» of the saint and the poet, he has endowed the act of thinking as a «pure act,» and the Self, considered transcendentally, has received attributes usually reserved for the divinity. For scholastic philosophy only the God of traditional religion is pure act, timeless and spaceless, productive of being. In actualistic idealism, man, concretely or transcendentally considered, shares this perfection. Nothing has any meaning unless constituted by the individual's act of thinking. Man doesn't simply know his world but, like God, he creates it. Man's act of knowing and willing are one and the same because of the simplicity of spirit. In knowing God we love Him, and He comes within us. God is Truth. Yet, truth is to be found within, and it is man's act of thinking which absolutely and concretely generates truth. When a man says: «I think that God exists,» God is discovered in the mediateness of this thinking act which is also constitutive or creative of God.[3] Agnosticism can only be a profession of ignorance.[4] The Self

[2] *Ibid.*, p. 248: «L'accusa di ateismo.»

[3] Cf. Chapter I, the section on «Truth.» See also *Discorsi di religione*, p. 140, where Gentile tells us that it is only «in a certain way» (in certo modo» that man creates God. It is man who is spirit,» not the ««natural man,» This text would apply here. Cr. *supra*, p. 55.

[4] *Introduzione alla filosofia*, pp. 20-23.

pronounces the truth of God with supreme authority. Being infinite and free, everything is immanent to it. It is my transcendental ego which makes me aware of myself as empirical and gives me awareness of my awareness, and so on ad infinitum.[5] A purely religious position would only weaken the value of man. Man must give God his value. This is the true and real humanism discovered by actualistic idealism. God will come alive within us. The human being is divinized by being what he is, i.e., act, not thing or fact. Materialism and naturalism are thus overcome by actualism.

Gentile believes that actualistic idealism is the philosophy for which men have been searching for centuries; that it brings the insight of St. Augustine to its zenith. By drawing man away from the «seductions» of modern empirical science, it responds to the «profound moral needs of our times which are universally orientated toward a reality which conforms to the aspirations of the spirit.»[6]

Gentile contends that it is the dualism brought about by transcendent metaphysics that causes atheism and agnosticism. Religion implies transcendence and dualism, while idealism implies immanence and unity, in fact, creative unity. How can a man be an atheist when his most profound humanity knows and loves truth which is an act of his very Self? Idealism teaches that God is immanent to this act of self-consciousness. The new God comes alive in this act. The history of Christianity which followed Augustine has tried to throw over the intellectual enchainment of Greek transcendence and find truth within our spiritual act, and so understand the words of St. Luke: «Ecce enim regnum Dei intra vos est» — the kingdom of God is within you.[7] Human history takes on a value here which the Greeks never even suspected. This human theogony (generation of God throughout history) is the substantial intuition of Christianity for Gentile.[8]

[5] *Ibid.*, pp. 20-23.

[6] *Ibid.*, p. 249.

[7] *I problemi della scolastica*, p. 39; scripture citation from Luke, XVII, 21.

[8] *Teoria generale dello spirito*, p. 265. Idealism sublimates the world in an eternal theogony which is fulfilled in our innermost being.

Gentile realized that his language had been misunderstood and in his *Introduction to Philosophy* made a careful effort to clarify matters. He explains that because he thinks of people in California, he does not make them to be or keep them in existence. Thought considered as limited, the thought of man empirically considered, cannot do this. The thought which thinks on its own limits and defines its limits cannot speak of itself as limited. This is thought for actualism. If, as empirical man, I think of God, I do not create Him. As much I am only creature among the other creatures of nature. On the other hand, the good Christian who has searched for God in his own breast, in his own thought, «is the one who sees man as both divine and eternal...» [9] The method of immanence teaches that just because we speak of subjectivity, we do not necessarily speak of the non-real. To presume that all reality is extra-subjective is to beg the question. The idealist can speak of the objectivity of God, but he means objectivity relative to a subject. When one posits the extra-subjective, he has also posited a postulate of the subject, and this can lead to nothing which is outside the subject. [10]

What then is God for Gentile? He is the objective moment of thinking which is dialectical, but as such He always escapes thinking, as Gentile conceives it, because thinking can never catch up with itself. In this sense He is never completely and finally interiorized, and therefore we cannot speak of God as absolutely immanent to thought. From these texts we have seen that God is immanent to the world. He is «at the core of things and men.» He is to be found in the laws of nature. God is discovered as a profound moral *need* as man constantly seeks to overcome his finite condition. [11] We feel our own condition as finite; we feel and recognize His intellig-

[9] *Introduzione alla filosofia,* p. 252.

[10] *Ibid.,* p. 253.

[11] Carlini saw this when he wrote: «In realtà, quell'assoluto immanentismo era soltanto un attegiamento polemico contro un concetto errato della trascendenza: ...la trascendenza che non era radicata nel seno stesso dell'immanenza, ossia che non rispondesse a un *bisogno* insoprimibile dello spirito nella sua interiorità.» Cf. *supra,* p. 30.

ence in the world. Thus while Gentile strives to overcome what for him is the exaggerated transcendence of religion and abstract logic, his God is not as immanent as he would have Him, nor as immanent as Gentile's critics have considered Him to be, i.e., so immanent that His real, transcendent existence is implicitly denied.

Therefore, Gentile's God is supposedly the new God, the God who lives in the heart and thought of every actualistic idealist. What He is in Himself is a dead abstraction, it doesn't matter (even though whatever man is, whatever man can do, is the result of God's creative act). The modern God of the actualistic idealist, the God created by the pure act of thinking into which all reality is subsumed, this is the God of modern man. This is the God of Giovanni Gentile, and it is the Transcendental Ego which gives Him this life and value. One may call the theory agnosticism or blasphemy. In any case it is the result of sincere effort to resolve long-standing dualisms.

# BIBLIOGRAPHY

## 1.- WRITINGS OF GENTILE

### (a) Books

*Polemica hegeliana,* Napoli: Pierro e Veraldi, 1902.

*La rinascita dell'idealismo,* Napoli: T. della r. Università, 1903.

*Giordano Bruno nella storia della cultura,* Milano: Remo Saudron, 1907.

*Il modernismo e i rapporti fra religione e filosofia,* Bari: Laterza, 1909.

*I problemi della scolastica e il pensiero italiano,* Bari: Laterza, 1913.

*La riforma della dialettica hegeliana,* Messina: Principato, 1913.

*Le origini della filosofia contemporanea in Italia,* 4 Vol. Messina: Principato, 1917.

*Sistema di logica come teoria del conoscere,* Pisa: Spoerri, 1918.

*L'esperienza pura e la realta storica,* Firenze: Sansoni, 1918.

*Il tramonto della cultura sicliana,* Bologna: Zanichelli, 1919.

*Bertrando Spaventa,* Firenze: Vallecchi, 1920.

*Saggi critici,* Seria Prima, Napoli: Ricciardi, 1921.

*Saggi critici,* Seria Seconda, Firenze: Vallecchi, 1927.

*Scritti filosofici,* Bari: Laterza, 1922.

*General Theory of the Spirit as Pure Act,* Tr. by H. Wildon Carr, London, Macmillan, 1922.

*Il modernismo e i rapporti fra religione e filosofia,* 2nd. ed. Bari: Laterza, 1922.

*Che cosa è il fascismo?* Firenze: Vallecchi, 1925.

*Il pensiero italiano del secolo 19: discorso,* Milano: Treves, 1928.

(ed.), *Enciclopedia italiana di scienze, lettere e arti,* Roma, 35 vol., 1929-1937.

*La riforma della scolastica,* Firenze: Sansoni, 1925.

*Opere complete,* Milano: Treves, 1928. Vol. I.

*Giambattista Vico,* Firenze: Sansoni, 1936.

*L'atto del pensare come atto puro,* Firenze: Sansoni, 1937.

*Dottrina politica del fascismo,* Padova: Milani, 1937.

*Il pensiero italiani del rinascimento,* 3rd. ed. Firenze: Sansoni, 1940.

*Sistema di logica,* 2 vols. 3rd. ed. Firenze: Sansoni, 1940.

*La mia religione,* Firenze; Sansoni, 1940.

*Sommario di pedagogia,* 2 vols. 5th. ed., Firenze: Sansoni, 1942.

*Genesi e struttura della societa,* Firenze: Sansoni, 1946.

*Introduzione alla filosofia,* 2nd. ed. Firenze: Sansoni, 1952.

*Rosmini e Gioberti,* Firenze: 1955. Doctoral thesis, 1897.

*Discorsi di religione,* 4th. ed. Firenze: Sansoni, 1957.
*Teoria generale dello spirito come atto puro,* 6th ed. Firenze, Sansoni, 1959.
*Genesis and Structure of Society,* Tr. by H. S. Harris, Urbana, Ill.; U. of Ill. Press, 1960.
*I fondamenti della filosofia del diritto,* 3rd. ed. Firenze Sansoni, 1961.
*Il modernismo e i rapporti fra religione e filosofia,* Firenze: Sansoni, 1962.
*Storia della filosofia italiana,* 2nd. ed. Firenze: Sansoni, 1962.
*Storia della filosofia,* Firenze: Sansoni, 1963.

(b) Articles

«Il problema della filosofia della storia.» *Atti del Congresso Internazionale di Scienze Storiche,* 1903.
«Il regno dello spirito,» *Cultura,* n. 4, 1909.
«Arte e religione,» *Giornale critico della filosofia,* n. 2, 1910.
«La scolastica e il prof. de Wulf,» *Critica,* n. 1. 1908.
«Idealismo e misticismo,» *Annurario della biblioteca filosofica di Palermo,* n. 3-4, 1914.
«Panlogismo,» *Giornale critico della filosofia italiana,* n. 1, 1921.
«Realismo e idealismo,» *Giornale critico della filosofia italiana,* n. 1, 1921.
«Il dialettismo,» *Giornale critico della filosofia italiana,* n. 3, 1921.
«Il mio ateismo e la storia del cristianesimo,» *Giornale critico della filosofia italiana,* n. 4, 1922.
«Art and Religion,» *Revue de Metaphysique et de Morale,* n. 4, 1923.
«Intorno all'idealismo attuale,» *La Voce,* Vol. 5 (1924), pp. 269-279.
«I tomisti italiani,» *Giornale critico della filosofia italiana,* n. 2, 1924.
«Intorno alla logica della concreto,» *Giornale critico della filosofia italiana,* n. 3, 1924.
«La riforma scolastica,» *Discorso,* Firenze, 1925.
«Contro l'agnosticismo della scuola,» *La coronazione della Scuola,* n. 1, 1925.
«Spinoza e la filosofia italiana,» *Chronicum Spinozanum,* Vol. V, 1927.
«Il problema religiosa in Italia,» *Educazione fascista,* Vol. V (1927), pp. 5-24.
«Attualismo e cattolicesimo,» *Giornale critico della filosofia italiana,* n. 6, 1930.
«I fondamenti dell'idealismo attuale,» *Nuova Antologia,* Vol. CCCLVI (1931), pp. 300-310.
«La concezione umanistica del mondo,» *Nuova Antologia,* Vol. CCCLV (1931), pp. 307-317.
«Eternità e storicità della filosofia,» *Giornale critico della filosofia italiana,* n. 2, 1931.
«Di una nuova dimostrazione dell'esistenza di Dio,» *Annali Scuola Normale di Pisa,* 1932.
«Hegel e il pensiero italiano,» *Leonardo,* n. 5, 1933.
«L'ultimo parola sull'attualismo,» *Giornale critico della filosofia italiana,* n. 2, 1934.

«Religione e filosofia nella scuola, Azione Cattolica,» *Giornale critico della filosofia italiana,* n. 3, 1934.

«Giudice su Benedetto Croce,» *Riforma litteraria,* n. 9, 1937.

«Intorno al concetto di umanesimo,» *Giornale dantesco,* n. 28, 1937.

«La mia religione,» *Archivi di filosofia,* n. 3-4, 1943.

«Postille a 'La mia religione',» *Giornale critico della filosofia italiana,* n. 3, 1943.

«Documenti inediti sull'hegelismo napolitano,» Critica, n. 5-8, 1906; also in: Gentile, G., *Frammenti di storia della filosofia,* Lanciano, 1962.

## 2.- STUDIES ON GENTILE

ALBANESE, C., *Pensiero e realtà secondo attualismo,* Roma: Signorelli, 1926.

ALESSIO, Franco, *Studi sul neospiritualismo,* Milano: Bocca, 1953.

ALFIERI, V. E., «L'attualismo e la religione,» *Ricerche Religiose,* Sept. 1926, pp. 440-443; Jan. 1927, pp. 1-35.

BABOIS, Edward, «Genesis and Structure of Society,» *Revue Philosophique de Louvain* (1955), pp. 442-443.

BARTOLOMEI, T., *«L'idealismo italiano contemporanea esaminato alla luce della dottrina di San Tommaso,»* Torino.

BATTAGLIA, Felice, «La lezione spiritualistica di G. Gentile,» *Bibliofilia del giornale di metafisica,»* Vol. XII, 1955.

BELLEZZA, Vito, «Il limite esistentiale nell'«umanesimo di Giovanni Gentile,» *Giornale critico della filosofia italiana,* Vol. XXXIV (1955), pp. 433-462.

——, «Alterità e communicazione nel pensiero di Giovanni Gentile,» *Archives de Philosophie* (1950), pp. 45-67.

BIANCHI, Bianco, *Il problema religioso di Giovanni Gentile,* Firenze: La Nuova Italia, 1940.

BOAS, George, «Gentile and the Hegelian Invasion of Italy,» *Journal of Philosophy,* Vol. I (1926), pp. 184-188.

BONUCCI, A., «Lo spirito come oggetto; a proposito della filosofia del Gentile,» *Rivistatrimestrale di studi filosofici e religiosi,* Vol. I (1920), pp. 120-150.

BONTADINI, G., «Le polemiche dell'idealismo,» *Rivista di filosofia neo-scolastica,* n. 5-6, 1924; n. 6, 1925.

——, «L'idealismo e i neoscolastici,» *Giornale critico della filosofia italiana,* n. 6, 1926.

BOZZANI, L., «Sull'attualismo gentiliano,» *Rivista Rosminiana di Filosofia e di Cultura,* Vol. XXXII (1938), pp. 124-135.

BUSNELLI, G., «La realtà spirituale secondo il prof. Gentile,» *Civiltà Cattolica,* n. 1787, 1924; n. 1790, 1925.

——, «La religione tra il soggetto e il oggetto della conoscenza,» *Civiltà Cattolica,* n. 1794, 1925.

——, «L'atto puro del pensiero come svoglimento,» *Civiltà Cattolica,* n. 1798, 1925.

——, «Spirito e verità secondo il prof. Gentile, *Civiltà Cattolica,* n. 1800, 1925.

——, «L'unita e universalita del pensiero,» *Civiltà Cattolica,* n. 1806, 1925.

——, «I fondamenti dell'idealismo attuale esaminiti,» *Cività Cattolica,* 1926.

Calcaterra, C., «Una critica dell'idealismo di G. Gentile,» *Rivista di filosofia neoscolastico,* n. 5, 1923.

——, «On the so-called Identity of History and Philosophy,» *Philosophy and History,* (Oxford), 1936. Essay presented to Ernst Cassirer.

Carlini, Armondo, «Considerazioni su la logica del concreto di Giovanni Gentile,» *Giornale critico della filosofia italiana,* n. 1, 1924.

——, «Idealismo e spiritualismo,» *Giornale critico della filosofia italiana,* n. 4, 1924.

——, «Lo spirito come atto puro della personalità,» *La Nostra Scuola,* 1927.

——, «Caratteri generali dell'idealismo crociano-gentiliano,» *Studi gentiliani,* Vol. VIII (1958), pp. 67-74.

——, «Dall'immanenza alla trascendenza dell'atto in se,» *Studi gentiliani,* Vol. VIII (1958), pp. 37-45.

——, «Spiritualismo assoluto e spiritualismo cristiano,» *Studi gentiliani,* Vol. VIII (1958), pp. 97-101.

——, «Una nuova dimostrazione dell'essistanza di Dio,» *Studi gentiliani,* Vol. VIII (1958), pp. 349-366.

Catalisano, Lorenzo, «Intorno alla riforma della dialettica hegeliana di Giovanni Gentile,» *Giornale critico della filosofia italiana,* Vol. XXIX (1950), pp. 183-195.

Coli, G., «Intorno all'idealismo attuale,» *Giornale critico della filosofia italiana,* n. 1, 1933.

Cento, V., «Religione e morale nel pensiero di Giovanni Gentile,» *Bilychnis* (1923), p. 92.

Chiochetti, Emilio, *La filosofia di Giovanni Gentile,* Milano: Socièta Editrice, «Vita e Pensiero,» 1922.

Ciusa, Niso, «Sull'attualismo gentiliano in alcune recenti pubblicazioni,» *Rivista Internazionale di Filosofia del diritto,* Vol. XXXII (1955), pp. 365-372.

Cordovani, N., «Il tomismo di fronte al neo-idealismo,» *Acta,* 10 vols. Firenze: Sansoni, *Hebdomadae Thomisticae,* 1924.

——, «Actualismus Italicus et realismus S. Thomae,» *Angelicum,* Fasc. 4 (Oct.-Nov.-Dec., 1931), pp. 515-526.

Crespi, Angelo, «Actual Idealism — An Exposition of Gentile's Philosophy and its Practical Effects,» *Hibbert Journal,* Vol. XXV (1925/26), pp. 256-263.

——, «An Italian Philosophy of Absolute Immanence,» *Church* (1926), pp. 264-267.

CROCE, Benedetto, *Il caso Gentile e la disonestà nella vita universitaria* italiana, Sari: Laterza, 1909.

——, «Intorno all'idealismo attuale,» *La Voce,* Vol. V (Nov. 1913 and Jan. 1914), pp. 1195-1197; Vol. 6, n. 1, pp. 4-15.

D'AMATO, F., *Gentile,* Milano: Athena, 1926.

DE BURGH, W. G., «Gentile's Philosophy of Spirit,» *Journal of Philosophical Studies,* Vol. IV (1929), pp. 3-22.

DE SANTILLANA, Giorgio, «The Idealism of Giovanni Gentile,» *Isis,* Vol. XXIX (1938), pp. 366-376.

DE SARLO, Francesco, *Gentile e Croce,* Firenze: Le Monnier, 1925.

D'ORSI, Domenico, *Lo spirito come atto puro in Giovanni Gentile,* Padova: Cedam 1957.

——, «L'ultimo travestimento di Giovanni Gentile: L'attualismo cattolico,» *Sophia,* Vol. XXV (1957), pp. 185-198.

EVANS, Valmai, «The Philosophy of Giovanni Gentile,» *Personalist,* Vol. II (1930), pp. 185-192.

——, «The Ethics of Giovanni Gentile,» *Ethics,* Vol. XXXIX (1928/29), pp. 205-216.

FAUCCI, Dario, «La funzione del'sentimento nel pensiero di Giovanni Gentile,» *Giovanni Gentile: La Vita e il Pensiero,* Vol. V, Firenze, 1951, pp. 85-148.

FIORENTINO, Francesco, *Ritratti storici e saggi critici raccolti da G. Gentile,* Firenze: Sansoni, 1959.

GARIN, Eugenio, «Giovanni Gentile interprete del rinascimento,» *Giornale critico della filosofia italiana,* Vol. XXVI (1947), pp. 117-129.

GARNETT, A. C., «Giovanni Gentile'» *Australasian Journal of Psychology and Philosophy,* Vol. IV (1926), pp. 8-17.

GEMELLI, Agostino, «Necrologi: Giovanni Gentile,» *Rivista di filosofia Neo-Scolastica,* Vol. XXXVI (1944), pp. 69-74.

GENNARO, Emanuele, «Un fallito tentativo de critica dell'attualismo,» *Giovanni Gentile, La Vita e il pensiero,* Vol. V (1951), pp. 173-254.

GULLACE, G., «Gentile vs. Croce: a comparison of two rival aesthetic systems,» *Symposium,* Vol. XI (1957), pp. 75-91.

HARRIS, H. S., «Studi sull'attualismo e influenza di Gentile sulla cultura anglosassone,» *Giornale Critica della Filosofia Italiana,* Vol. XXXVIII (1959), pp. 312-342. English bibliography, pp. 342-352.

——, *The Social Philosophy of Giovanni Gentile,* Urbana, Ill.: Univ. of Ill. Press, 1960.

Holmes, Roger W., *The Idealism of Giovanni Gentile*, New York: Macmillan, 1937.

——, «Gentile's Sistema di Logica,» *Philosophical Review*, Vol. XL (1937), pp. 393-401.

Jacobelli, Isoldi, «La crisi dell'autocoscienza nella filosofia di Giovanni Gentile,» *Giornale Critico della Filosofia Italiana*, Vol. XXVII (1948), pp. 82-131.

La Via, V., *L'idealismo attuale di Giovanni Gentile*, Trani: Vecchi, 1925.

——, «L'attualismo come principio dell'autocritica dell'idealismo,» *Giornale critica della filosofia italiana*, n. 1 (1965), pp. 52-73.

——, «Soggetività e immanenza nel *Sistema di logica come teoria del conoscere*,» *Divus Thomas*, n. 2, 1925.

Lion, Aline, *The Idealistic Conception of Religion*, Oxford: Clarendon, 1932.

Lovecchio, Antonino, «La fase conclusiva di due filosofi,» *Rivista Filosofica*, Vol. VIII (1938), pp. 65-83.

LLugarini, Leo, «Il problema della logica nella filosofia di G. Gentile,» *Giovani Gentile: La vita e il pensiero*, Vol. VII (1954), Firenze, pp. 145-186.

Massolo, Arturo, «Gentile e la fondazione kantiana,» *Giornalecritico della filosofia italiana*, Vol. XXVI (1947), pp. 138-144.

Mattiusi, G., «L'idealismo in Italia,» *Gregorianum*, fasc. 2, 1920.

Mazzatini, Carlo, «La filosofia religiosa di Giovanni Gentile,» *La Scuola Cattolica*, Vol. LXXII (1944), pp. 81-99, 177-188.

Monaco, N., «La filosofia di Giovanni Gentile,» *Gregorianum*, fasc. 3 and 4, 1923.

Ottaviano, C., *Critica dell'idealismo*, Napoli: Rondinella, 1936.

Papini, G., «Giovanni Gentile,» *La Vraie Italie*, March, 1919.

Plebe, A., «Importanza del concetto gentilliano di inattualità dell'arte,» *Giornale critico della filosofia italiana*, Vol. XLIII, n. 3 (1964), pp. 327-332.

Pozzo, Gianni M., «Immanenza e transcendenza nel pensiero di Giovanni Gentile,» *Humanitas*, Vol. VIII (1953), pp. 467-474.

Proto, Pisani, «Il sentimento nella filosofia di Giovanni Gentile,» *Rivista di filosofia neo-scolastica*, Vol. XLV (Milano), pp. 329-339. (n.d.).

Raggiunti, Renzo, «Il concetto del tradurre nel pensiero di Giovanni Gentile,» *Giornale critico della filosofia italiana*, Vol. XXIX (1950), pp. 443-452.

Redano, Ugo, *La crisi dell'idealismo attuale*, Rome: Signorelli, 1924.

Romanelli, Patrick, *Croce versus Gentile, a Dialogue on Contemporary Italian Philosophy*, New York: S. F. Vanni, 1946.

——, *The Philosophy of Giovanni Gentile, an Inquiry into Gentile's Con-*

*ception of Experience*, New York: S. F. Vanni, 1938. First published as a Ph. D. thesis, 1937.

——, «A Possible Interpretation and an Appraisal of Giovanni Gentile,» *Sophia*, Vol. V (1937), pp. 384-392.

ROMOLO, Murri, «Religion and Idealism as Presented by Giovanni Gentile,» *Hibbert Journal*, Vol. XIX (1920/21), pp. 249-262.

SAITTA, Giuseppe, «Humanitas di Giovanni Gentile,» *Giornale critico della filosofia italiana*, Vol. XXVI (1947), pp. 62-73.

SANTARO, L., *Il problema di Dio nell'attualismo gentiliano*, Padova: Cedam, 1941.

SCHUWER, C., «La pensée italienne contemporaine; L'idealisme de Croce et de Gentile,» *Revue Philosophique*, Vol. XCVII, pp. 351-401; Vol. XCVII, pp. 82-123, 1924.

SCIACCA, Michele, *Trascendenza teistica e filosofia cristiana*, Torino, 1960.

——, «Il pensiero italiano del risorgimento ad oggi in libro di Giovanni Gentile, *Logos*, Vol. XXI (1938), pp. 440-443.

——, «Giovanni Gentile,» *Enciclopedia Cattolica*, Vol. VI (1951), pp. 32-36.

——, *La filosofia oggi*, 2 vols. Milano, 1958.

——, *Philosophical Trends in the Contemporary World*, Tr. by Attilio Salerno, Notre Dame, Indiana, Univ. Press, 1964.

SCOLERI, D., «La divina dialettica di Giovanni Gentile,» *Richerche filosofiche*,» Vol. XXII (1954), pp. 33-48.

SICHIROLLO, Livio, «Interiorità, trascendenza, metafisica appunta per una ripetizione del sistema gentiliano,» *Studi Urbaniti*, Vol. XXV (1951), pp. 102-116.

SMITH, J. A., «The Philosophy of Giovanni Gentile, *Proceedings of the Aristotelean Society*, Vol. XX (1919/20), pp. 63-78.

SPIRITO, Ugo, «Una critica della filosofia di G. Gentile,» *Nuova Antologia*, Vol. CCXXII (1923), pp. 350-358.

——, «La religione di Giovanni Gentile,» *Giovanni Gentile: La Vita e il Pensiero*, Vol. VII (1954), pp. 319-333.

——, «Giovanni Gentile,» *Enciclopedia Italiana*, Vol. XVI (1944), pp. 580-581.

——, «Giovanni Gentile,» *Enciclopedia Filosofica* (Roma-Venezia: Sansoni, 1957), Vol. II, pp. 631-643.

——, (ed.), *G. Gentile: La Vita e il Pensiero*, (10 vol.), Firenze.

VIGNA, C., «La dialettica gentiliana,» *Giornale critico della filosofia italiana*, Vol. XLIII, n. 3 (1964), pp. 362-392.

OBITUARY, *Journal of Philosophy*, Vol. XLII, Feb. 1945.

## 3.- OTHER STUDIES


COLLINS, James A., *A History of Modern European Philosophy*, Milwaukee, Wisc.: Bruce, 1951.

COPLESTON, Frederick, *A History of Philosophy*, Garden City, N.Y.: Doubleday, Vol. VII, 1965.

CRESPI, Angelo, *Contemporary Thought of Italy*, New York: A. A. Knopf, 1926.

FICHTE, Johann G., *The Vocation of Man*, (tr. by Roderick Chisholm), N. Y. C.: Bobbs-Merrill Co., 1956.

KAUFMAN, Walter, *Hegel*, Garden City, N.Y.: Doubleday, 1965.

MATCZAK, Sebastian A., *Karl Barth on God*, Staten Island, N.Y.: St. Paul Publications, 1962.

——, *Le problème de Dieu dans la pensée de Karl Barth*. Louvain: E. Nauwelaerts, 1968.

PELIZZI, Camillo, «The Problem of Religion for the Italian Idealists,» *Proceedings of the Aristotelean Society*, Vol. XXIX (1923/24), pp. 153-163.

SANTAYANA, Geo., *The German Mind*, T. Crowell Co., N.Y.C., 1968. (Originally published in 1915 as *Egotism in German Philosophy*).

SCHNEIDER, Herbert, *Making of the Fascist State*, New York: Oxford Univ. Press, 1928.

SMITH, Wm. A., *Twentieth Century Fascism*, New York: Monarch Press, 1965.

# INDEX OF NAMES

D/1970/0081/31

Printed in Belgium (1489)
by NAUWELAERTS, S.A., Printing Dept.